Canadian Financial Handbook
for Christian Living

Canadian
FINANCIAL
HANDBOOK
for
CHRISTIAN
LIVING

W. PAUL JOHNSON

Essence
PUBLISHING

Belleville, Ontario, Canada

Canadian Financial Handbook for Christian Living

Copyright © 1997, W. Paul Johnson

All Scripture quotations, unless otherwise specified, are taken from the *New International Version* of the Bible (Copyright © 1973, 1978, 1984 International Bible Society. Used by permission of Zondervan Bible Publishers. All rights reserved.)

ISBN: 1-896400-31-0

The author of this book is not held responsible for any errors, omissions or misunderstandings that result from this book. The information contained here is to be a practical guide to the general public and more specifically the Christian community. Individual circumstances will vary. You are encouraged throughout this book to obtain further counsel from your financial institution, financial advisor, accountant, broker, lawyer or other professional. Always research thoroughly and understand what you are doing before any final decisions are made about your personal finances.

Essence Publishing is a Christian Book Publisher dedicated to furthering the work of Christ through the written word. For more information, contact:
103B Cannifton Rd., Belleville, ON, Canada K8N 4V2.
Phone: 1-800-238-6376. Fax: (613) 962-3055.
Email: essence@intranet.on.ca
Internet: http://www.essence.on.ca

Printed in Canada
by

Essence
PUBLISHING

DEDICATION

This book is dedicated to my two sons,
Ross and Taylor.

SPECIAL THANKS

First and foremost I want to thank my wife and family for their
patience while I wrote this book. My wife has been especially
encouraging in motivating me throughout the writing
process by her prayers and words. To Neal Black, a
special thank you for providing feedback and
direction to me all along the way. I must
thank my parents. My mother attempted to teach me how to manage
money at a young age with
my allowance. Who
would have thought
that now I am
teaching
others!
There are also
family & friends
who have been praying
that God would give me
guidance as I wrote this book.
Special thanks to Peter and Kim
Phillips and Brian and Margaret Penner
for your unfailing friendship and prayers as
we remember you and your families in our daily
prayers. *Great is the Lord and most worthy of praise; His*
greatness no one can fathom. One generation will commend Your
works to another; they will tell of Your mighty acts (Psalm 145:3-4).

ABOUT THE AUTHOR

Paul Johnson has been in the banking and financial industry for over eight years employed with both the Royal Bank of Canada and Canada Trust over this time frame. He graduated from Trinity Western University in Langley, BC with a B.A. in Business Administration. He also has a two-year diploma in Biblical Studies from Northwest Baptist Theological College.

Originally from London, Ontario where his father built many houses and churches and then pastored at various churches throughout Ontario, Paul has been in British Columbia now for almost fifteen years. He has settled with his wife and two sons in the Comox Valley area of Vancouver Island, British Columbia.

Table of Contents

$ $ $

SECTION THREE: BORROWING MONEY – PERSONAL LENDING

SECTION FOUR: BORROWING MONEY – MORTGAGES

SECTION FIVE: WILLS, WEALTH & WHATEVER

APPENDIX

Preface

$ $ $

I have been involved in the personal or retail banking industry in Canada for about eight years. Over the past five years, the idea of this resource book has been constantly on my mind, but not until now have I been so strongly led by God to actually start and complete it. Recently, my family was at a week long family camp where the speaker's final message was on God's will. The speaker gave many examples of how we need to take our gifts and use them to God's glory. We need to follow God's direction through reading His Word and prayer. We also need to take the advice of other Christians as a form of direction. In the conversations I've had with many Christians over the years, I have always been encouraged to pursue the writing of this book. In fact, the same day as this message, two Christian couples encouraged me to pursue writing because they see my conviction as a need that must be filled. God has given me specific gifts, knowledge, experience, conviction and direction, which I must use to His glory for the benefit of Christians across Canada. 1 Peter 4:10 states, *Each one should use whatever gift he has received to serve others, faithfully administering God's grace in its various forms.*

Just as Christians need to learn about topics such as God's will, prayer, end times, etc., they also need information and guidance about their personal finances. If you enter your local Christian bookstore, you are hard pressed to find financial resources that are exclusive to Canada. You will find some excellent material written by American authors, but their audience is specifically the United States. The financial and banking industry in Canada is very different from that of our neighbours to the south.

My conviction has been to fill this void and supply Christians who are Canadian with a practical resource guide to help them better understand (knowledge), manage (experience) and plan (direction) their personal finances. This book will not concentrate specifically on the biblical applications of personal finance, even though references are made to the Bible. Currently, there are a number of authors who have excellent resources available on the biblical teachings of finance that you should also consider reading.

As a banker, I see a variety of clientele. Some are just starting out on their own or as a newly married couple. Others are trying to cope with a debt load that they feel is beyond their means while at the same time trying to figure out how they got into this spiraling predicament. Still others are raising children and attempting to balance what the real "needs" and "wants" for the family are. Then there are those who are approaching retirement or already retired. They aren't sure if they will have enough funds and income to survive the uncertain future.

The topic of personal finance is rarely taught in the church, though this is not the fault of the pastor. Other than their own personal lives, what knowledge or experience do they have on this topic since it is not part of their formal training? Unfortunately, however, stress related to finances leads to other struggles in the home and work which could lead flocks to seek counsel from their pastor or spiritual mentor. This book is not intended to solve these or other problems that people face with their finances. However, it may help for both pastors and individuals in the congregation to better understand the financial industry when providing or seeking counseling.

One of the key reasons for this book is to provide information for you to educate yourself on personal finances. When you reflect on your schooling, whether it be public, Christian or home schooling, you will recall being taught various subjects such as history, science and math. Some schools are currently teaching our young people about finances, but very few. And for those that are, do the teachers have the knowledge, experience and tools necessary to teach on this topic? How did you figure out what a chequing account was or an RSP? Most of us learn it by trial and error. Even then we are unsure if we really had and still have the knowledge to make those decisions. Why? Because no one really took the time to explain and teach basic principles of finances. At a young age, my mother tried to teach me how to manage my allowance. At the time, I may not have understood why, but now I am grateful. What about the next generation? If you think the current economic uncertainties in your life are stressful and confusing, what help is there for your children and their children?

You may find in portions of this book areas where you will need to approach your personal accountant, broker, lawyer, financial advisor or other professional for more specific information as it relates to you personally.

Use this book as a practical guide or handbook to: 1) help you be a good steward of what God has given you; 2) help you educate yourself; and 3) help you plan your future. If this takes place, then you will be prepared to counsel others so that they also will be good stewards and witnesses of what God has given to them.

SECTION ONE
Day-To-Day Personal Finances

$ $ $

Topics covered here relate to what happens in your personal finances on a daily basis. Some chapters, like budgeting, aren't something you do on a daily basis; however, it directly relates to what you do with your finances on a daily basis.

"Therefore I tell you, do not worry about your life, what you will eat or drink; or about your body, what you will wear. Is not life more important than food, and the body more important than clothes? Look at the birds of the air; they do not sow or reap or store away in barns, and yet your heavenly Father feeds them. Are you not much more valuable than they? Who of you by worrying can add a single hour to his life? ...So do not worry, saying, 'What shall we eat?' or 'What shall we wear?' For the pagans run after all these things, and your heavenly Father knows that you need them. But seek first His Kingdom and His righteousness, and all these things will be given to you as well. Therefore do not worry about tomorrow, for tomorrow will worry about itself. Each day has enough trouble of its own."

Matthew 6:25-27, 31-34

And my God will meet all your needs according to His glorious riches in Christ Jesus. To our God and Father be glory for ever and ever. Amen.

Philippians 4:19-20

Your Bank Account

$ $ $

Basically, there are two types of bank accounts – savings and chequing. Each Financial Institution (FI) may call it by their own special title or name, but it all really boils down to two account types.

SAVINGS ACCOUNT

As the name implies, this is where you put your hard earned savings. This is not an account from which you make a lot of withdrawals or write a lot of cheques. If you do make withdrawals from this account, expect to pay higher fees in service charges. The charge per item is usually greater on this account in comparison to a chequing account because the FI is also paying you interest income on the funds you have on deposit. If interest rates are extremely low, you won't be earning a lot of interest on your money unless you have a lot of money on deposit. Therefore, your interest won't come close to paying for the service charges. When interest rates are much higher, people are happy when the interest earned pays for the service charges. Be careful. Even if interest rates pay for your service charges, you should still make sure you are being a good steward. Make sure you are in the correct account type for the purpose you have the account for in the first place. The interest you do earn is usually paid to you at the end of each month. That means for the next month you will earn interest on your interest, etc. This is called compounding interest which means you earn interest on your interest each month.

If you have savings in USD (United States Dollars), then consider a US Savings Account. By depositing US money to a US Savings account, you avoid the exchange rate both when depositing and when withdrawing your funds. In other words, if you deposit $10US today, you will receive $10US when you withdraw it no matter if the exchange rates were different on each date. Check into any service charges on the USD accounts as they are usually payable in USD funds and not Canadian funds.

CHEQUING ACCOUNT

Again, as the word states, this account is for writing cheques. This is the account from which a majority of all your transactions should come, including cheques, withdrawals, bill payments, electronic debit memos (this means you have authorized a company to take a specific amount of money out of your account on a specific day each month, such as life insurance premiums, etc.). This is your day-to-day account. You could have your mortgage and loan payments come from here. If you have access to direct deposit of your paycheque to your bank account, then it is suggested your mortgage and loan payments come from this account. Some people like more than one chequing account for various reasons. That is fine as long as you can administer all your accounts without confusion or error (such as a Non-Sufficient Funds cheque because you wrote the cheque on the wrong account, which is very embarrassing). Consider and compare how much extra service charges are being taken from you in justifying the extra account(s). Some chequing accounts do pay a little interest on the daily balance; however, that isn't the sole purpose of the account so don't expect much (that is what the savings account is for).

Some FI's have USD chequing accounts. Most people don't need this type of account, but if you see a need for it then ask your FI. One word of caution, as stated in the Savings Account section above, is that usually the service charges payable are collected by the FI as USD funds and not CAD (Canadian Dollars) funds.

PACKAGE ACCOUNTS

For this next section you should locate your chequing passbook or statements for the last three months. Look specifically at the month end and you should find your various service charges. There may be other service charges that have taken place during the month also, but the majority of them will be at the month end.

If you notice your service charges are quite high, you should approach your FI to see if they have any package accounts that could save you money (again, being a good steward). Currently, many FI's have more than one package account because their customers have different needs. The package account is usually attached to or "placed over" the customer's chequing account. This means that instead of paying on a per item basis, you pay a specific monthly fee that will cover various items that the package offers, depending on the package you choose and the various features it offers. Think of the package as various features with specific benefits at a certain cost to you. That is why you must study what your FI offers to determine what is of most benefit to your own personal needs. Some packages let you write a certain number of cheques per month, including withdrawals, plus other banking products such as traveller's cheques, money orders, bank drafts, etc.

You need to review your service charges over the past three months and approach your FI for account package information even if you have already put a package on your account. Why? Banking is becoming very competitive and new products and services are offered without you even knowing it. If you don't ask and keep up to date, then the account package type you have now may not be the package type you really need. There might be something better for you.

The opposite could also be true here. Maybe you are currently paying for an account package when, if you break down your items, it would be cheaper to pay on a per item basis instead.

To be innovative and provide products that customers are requesting, many FI's have special accounts for the very young, youth and students. If you are a senior, which is defined differently at every FI (starting age from 55 to 60), be sure you are in a senior's package account. It will save you money in service charges and it could also give you other benefits.

SERVICE CHARGES

You need to look at all the service charges you pay. If you do not understand them, then ask for help from your FI. You should be able to break down your service charges as per the activity that took place previously during the month. As stated earlier, you must obtain from your FI their most recent publication on their service charges. Many FI's will charge you more for doing your withdrawals with a live teller/officer than if you went to their bank machine or used another type of automation. If you pay your bills through the bank machine, over the telephone banking or now on your home PC, you may be charged differently than if you saw a live teller.

FI's are encouraging you to use the automation provided instead of the wicket. They will normally reward you with less service charges if you take this route. I can't comment on whether this is right or wrong as everyone has varied opinions about it. However, there is a large cost to the FI to operate a branch (especially the employee expense). In years to come, a gradual diminish in the teller focus will occur in favour of the automation focus. Again, each FI has a different mission statement and objectives, so one FI may be going towards reduced tellers available (which if you use them will cost you more and you will have to wait longer to see one), while the other FI may have a different focus to reduce its costs. Simply be aware of the differences between automation service charges and other types of service charges.

A newer service charge you will see has to do with purchasing goods/services electronically instead of using cash. No doubt you have seen the commercials about this. For those who are unfamiliar with this, you can purchase your groceries, a pair of jeans or maybe even this book by using your bank card instead of cash. The system electronically transfers the money to purchase the goods/services from your account at your FI to the account of the merchant's FI automatically and immediately. Often this transaction will cost you less in service charges than writing a cheque or withdrawing the cash from the bank machine. Is this type of a transaction leading to a cashless society? I will discuss that topic a little later in this book for those interested.

One bit of information that could save you enough money to pay for this book is this: Be careful when you use a bank machine that is not from the FI you bank at when withdrawing money. Every time you do this it will cost you. If you do a lot of this, look again at your passbook or statement, as often this service charge is listed separately from your other regular service charges. Some FI's include these in a package account, so again, do some research about your FI. In my banking experience, I have seen a customer pay over $100.00 in one month for this one item. That means that in the previous month, they went to another FI's bank machine over 3 times per day on average! Try to use your own FI's bank machines whenever possible even when traveling. If you have no other choice, then be smart about how often you withdraw because each one of these starts to add up. This is money you could use for other needs or another's need if you simply took the time to find your FI's bank machine.

Of course, a service charge you should always avoid is NSF cheques (Non-Sufficient Funds) or NSF EDM's (Electronic Debit Memos). It is not only embarrassing, but it is also a poor witness of your being a Christian to both the FI and the person to whom the cheque was written. Consider a small overdraft facility in case of human error or when, at month end, the FI collects your service charges and now there isn't enough funds to cover your cheque. More about overdraft facilities a little later. However, we need to be careful as we are witnesses of Christ in all we do, including how we handle our bank accounts.

WORKSHEET

Gather those passbooks/statements and let's start the research. Make sure you have that current publication of what your FI's service charges are for each item type and what package types they offer. Provided for you is a worksheet to help you get started. Modify it to your own needs by adding to it if necessary or moving items around. Compare and hopefully you can save some money. You can also use this worksheet to compare one FI with another FI if you are considering changing FI's.

In a one month time-frame:

Banking Item Costing:	#	Cost/Item	Total $	
# of cheques written				
# of withdrawals made (live teller)				
# of withdrawals made (automation)				
# of bills paid (live teller)				
# of bills paid (automation)				
# of transfers of $ from this acct.				
# of electronic transfers/debit memos				
# of money orders/bank drafts				
# of times used another FI's bank machine				
# of times bought goods electronically				
# of times purchased traveller's cheques				
# of times charged for overdraft protection				
# of certified cheques				
Is there any record keeping fee on the acct?				
If statement, do you pay each month for it?				
Do you pay for cancelled cheques returned?				
Other items:				
#				
#				
#				
#				
#				
Total Cost per Month: (A)	#=		$	(A)
Account Service Package Cost at FI:			$	
Extra items above Service Package:				
#				
#				
#				
#				
#				
Total Cost per Month (B)			$	(B)
Subtract (B) from (A) to get (C)	(A)=			
	(B)=			
	(C)=			

If (C) is negative then stay with the pay as you go per item method.
If (C) is positive then consider changing to the service package method.

Deposit Insurance

$ $ $

Banks, trust and loan companies are chartered through the Federal Government and the Credit Unions through the Provincial Governments.

If you bank at a Credit Union, I would suggest that you approach your branch about this topic to ensure that you are properly educated. Each province may have different policies regarding deposit insurance. They do have brochures and contact phone numbers to help you further, so ask.

For the banks, trust and loan companies, your deposits are covered by what is referred to as CDIC (Canada Deposit Insurance Corporation) coverage as long as your bank, trust or loan company is a member of CDIC. CDIC is an arm of the Federal Government which will guarantee depositors their funds up to certain limitations and restrictions if one of its members fails. CDIC has produced two helpful brochures. The first brochure lists out all its current members. If your FI is not listed here, then phone CDIC and make sure they didn't recently join. If you discover after the phone call that they are still not a member of CDIC, then further research with your FI is necessary. The second brochure provides very useful information about CDIC coverage. I suggest you request a copy of each brochure for yourself from your FI. You can also request the same information directly from CDIC by calling 1-800-461-CDIC (2342) or writing to:

CDIC
50 O'Connor Street
17th Floor
P.O. Box 2340, Station D
Ottawa, Ontario K1P 5W5

In the 1980s and 1990s, there have been a few trust company failures. One in particular out of Alberta revealed that the main trust company was CDIC insured; however, they were also selling RSP and other deposit instruments to the public through two subsidiary companies which, while owned by the parent company that was insured by CDIC, were not themselves listed as insured under CDIC. Therefore, when the subsidiary companies failed, the depositors were not guaranteed anything. So, be careful and get educated.

Overdraft Protection

$ $ $

Previously, I mentioned that, in order to avoid the embarrassment of writing an NSF cheque, you should consider setting up a reasonable overdraft facility on your chequing account. There are a couple of things to note here, however. I said "reasonable" limit. You should be able to revolve from the negative to the positive on a paycheque-by-paycheque basis as a maximum limit. However, the overdraft should really be for those times when a miscalculation has taken place in your cheque register and you want to ensure your cheque will be honoured when it clears your account. It is a safety measure.

You must remember that when you are in overdraft, you now owe money; it is a debt that must be repaid. You don't want to be so far into overdraft that even when you get paid you are still in the overdraft, or negative balance. If this is the case, consider talking to your FI about a loan with a definite repayment plan, since this would be at a lesser interest rate than what you are paying on your overdraft facility. You will have to compare the interest rates of the overdraft to a small loan, or Line of Credit (LOC). Some FI's will charge a higher interest rate for small loans under a specific dollar amount. However, if the overdraft is costing you 21% and the loan is going to cost you prime plus 6% (prime rate in this example = 7%), you are saving 8% in interest charges and, at the same time, repaying back the overdraft with regular payments. If you have other debts that also need consolidating, then this would be the time to do it with the new loan or Line of Credit... more on that topic later.

In summary, have a small overdraft set up as a safety measure to avoid embarrassment. Make sure the overdraft at minimum revolves from pay to pay. Make sure your debt is at the cheapest interest rate possible if you are heavily into an overdraft that you can't climb out of.

Your Bank Card

$ $ $

Bank card refers to the plastic card that you use as a form of identification to your FI, in the bank machine to withdraw money or for doing telephone banking transactions. Each FI calls the card by a different name, so for simplicity's sake we will refer to it as a bank card. One very important thing to be very aware of is the privacy of your PIN (personal identification number). Under no circumstances do you ever give this code to anyone, even if someone calls you and says they are from your FI and just need to confirm your PIN. Your FI will never ask you for your PIN. This is confidential information. When you enter your PIN at a branch, tellers on the other side of the counter don't know what your actual PIN is – they simply see characters such as "****." If someone were to phone you asking for your PIN, report this to your FI immediately. There have been cases of bank cards going missing in the mail and a con-artist tricking unsuspecting customers into giving their PIN and then withdrawing money from their account. Also, if your bank card is lost or stolen, report it immediately to your FI. So, be careful and aware of keeping your bank card PIN confidential and secure.

The bank card has revolutionized banking, and you haven't seen anything of its capabilities yet. Very few customers do not carry their FI's bank card. In banking, it opens the doors to what is referred to as "alternate distribution" methods of banking. By using your bank card to complete a transaction, it is less costly to the FI than providing personnel in the branch network.

As you may know, you can do the following with your bank card:

• withdraw money from your account by using either your FI's bank machine or another FI's bank machine;

- do many other transactions at the bank machine, and with time, the types of transactions will expand to include items such as traveller's cheques and USD cash to name a few;

- use telephone banking facilities by either talking with a live operator or completing your transactions by touch-tone automation;

- some FI branches require you to swipe your card at the wicket to bring up your portfolio;

- purchase goods and services at a store, which many people refer to as a debit card;

- for those FI's that offer it, computer banking on your home PC through FI-supplied software;

- again, for those FI's that offer it, computer banking through the Internet for both product information and credit applications.

What is the future of the plastic bank card? Many of our major Canadian FI's are working together with foreign banks from around the world on further enhancements to the bank card. There are various trade names which I can't mention here, but I can tell you what their goals are. Testing is currently under way to allow you to access with your bank card all of the above, as well as your credit card, Line of Credit and cash.

How do you access cash? Instead of approaching the bank machine to withdraw pieces of paper we call "money," you will approach the bank machine and "load" your card with cash up to the amount you want to carry. When you approach a retailer to purchase an item, you will have a choice of how you want to pay: "Will that be 'plastic cash,' credit card, debit card or your line of credit?" Are we heading for a "cashless" society? That depends on what your definition of "cashless" is. Nevertheless, the Bible states that the world is heading towards a cashless globe, so don't be surprised if banking is heading that direction as well. You will see the magnetic strip on the back of your bank card replaced by a computer chip. This has significant ramifications because the computer chip can hold immense amounts of information. Keep your eye on what is happening with computers and banking and you will see that banking is definitely on the electronic super-highway.

The FI's like the idea of no more paper cash because this will dramatically reduce both their expenses in handling cash and fraud write-offs. Utilizing "computer cash," or what I referred to above as "plastic cash," through electronic distribution has the potential to eliminate cheque-writing also. Sound far-fetched? The computer industry is changing our lives daily. It will affect each one of us more and more every day, even if we don't realize its actual effects. The banking industry will be an integral part of this change.

Before all of you destroy your bank card, I want to make something clear. I believe the bank card is part of the process towards a cashless society; however, there is more to come before the world arrives at its godless goals. May I encourage you not to worry about this if it troubles you, because no matter what your view is on eschatology, God is in control. Always worship and glorify Him. The banking industry will be involved in the end times just like other industries will be involved. This discussion is to get you thinking, since none of us has control over the future – only our God does, so trust Him. We are commanded to *"watch and pray"* in Matthew 26:41, and in Mark 13:32-33, Jesus says, *"No one knows about that day or hour, not even the angels in heaven, nor the Son, but only the Father. Be on guard! Be alert! You do not know when that time will come."*

Economists

$ $ $

If you read the newspaper, listen to the radio or watch the news, you will hear reports about our economy as well as the economies of other countries – especially the USA and Japan – almost on a daily basis. You will hear more about the "global" economy as time goes on, since world economies are becoming more globally-minded. So, too, is the banking industry becoming globally-minded. That is why Return on Equity of our large FI's is now compared to that of large FI's in other countries as a benchmark of where they stand globally. It is not enough to just compete at home.

These people called economists analyze information relating to our economy. Depending on how they analyze data, they come up with a conclusion about an economy. In many ways, they are trying to predict the future like the weatherperson on television predicts what the weather will be tomorrow or three days from now. In two different newspapers dated the same day, you may find two different conclusions by two different economists using the exact same data. One economist may say the economy will grow over the next year while another says it will shrink.

You must understand that theirs is an opinion based on interpretation of certain facts and biases. Their opinions are not absolute fact. Therefore, read, listen and watch what the economists state, for their opinions are really quite useful. However, be careful in how you apply what they say to your personal finances.

In my work, there are many times when customers ask me if I think mortgage interest rates will continue to go down or if they should lock in for 5 years now; or, do I think they should take out that investment certificate for only 30 days or lock in for the whole year? I can give my opinion, but I always qualify it with a disclaimer statement that I really don't know the answer the customer is seeking because anything is possible. In my banking career, I have seen prime rate spike up 2% overnight, which shocked a lot of people. You have to take the data, the opinions of the economists or personal financial advisors (if you want to know their opinion, of course) and come to your own conclusions. It is your money after all.

Safe Deposit Box

$ $ $

In the FI's vault are a lot of different sized compartments with locks on each of them. Other than where the money is locked up, these compartments are called safe deposit boxes. You can rent a box from your FI if they have any available. They come in sizes of small, medium and large. There could be special sizes also available at certain branches.

By renting a safe deposit box (SDB), you can store or "safekeep" your personal valuables in a safe place away from your home or business. Important documents, precious metals, jewelry, coins and your will are some of the many items you can store in a SDB. Depending on how much you have to store will determine the size of box you will need. The rental charge on the SDB is one of the few items in banking on which you will pay GST. Because you are "renting" the SDB, the government has determined that it is a service and therefore must be taxed under the GST legislation. Don't be surprised when you are told this by the bank officer. You should also be aware that the rent you pay on your SDB is currently allowed as an income tax deduction (check your Income Tax Guide or talk with your accountant) and normally, you do not need an official bank receipt to claim it on your taxes.

The registration on who can access your SDB can be set up in different ways. The simplest method is Sole Proprietor (Owner). This means that only you can enter your SDB, giving you plenty of privacy. However, when you die, your next of kin or estate will have to go to the courts to get a judge's authority to enter your box. If they cannot locate your key to the SDB, then the box will have to be drilled upon execution of the court order with this expense falling on the estate. If this concerns you, then you may want to consider one of the following alternatives.

Joint Tenants means that more than one person is signed on the box's rental agreement, but any one of the tenants is allowed to enter the box without the knowledge or consent of any of the other persons signed on the agreement. Many times a husband and wife will rent a SDB this way. It makes for ease of entry to the SDB by either party, and in the event of death of one partner, the other can still enter the box on his or her own.

Joint Tenants in Common means that more than one person is signed on the box's rental agreement, but both or any two of the signed parties must be present at the FI at the same time to sign to enter the SDB. The SDB is handed to both parties to enter and both parties must hand the box back to the FI's officer to be placed back in the locked compartment. Both people must be present with that box at all times, otherwise the "in Common" part of the agreement is breached. Husband and wife can set up the rental agreement this way, but when one partner dies, the other would have to obtain court approval to enter the box. Businesses will often set up a SDB this way to ensure proper custody of the box's contents.

Agency agreement is another method, though not used that often, by which you can set up your SDB rental agreement. This means that you are allowing another individual, usually your lawyer or executor, access to the contents of your SDB. You must really trust whoever you give this right to because they are acting on your behalf as if it were you there personally.

In case of fire, theft or misplaced items, it is a good idea to have a SDB. They are relatively inexpensive. Of course, you can only enter your SDB during open hours of operation of the FI's branch. Don't go overboard on what you store in the box either. I had a customer come in upset that he had lost his key to his SDB. I explained that when we rent out a SDB, we give the customer two keys (which we are to test in front of the customer in the vault to make sure both are correct), so does he remember where his spare key might be? He smiled and then frowned. You see, he decided that the safest place to store his extra key was in his SDB. Needless to say, he had to pay for the box to be drilled and a new lock attached.

Chequing Account Reconciliation

$ $ $

This is a task which many of us don't do simply because it takes time and we get frustrated easily. However, if you don't reconcile, or balance, your accounts monthly, then do you know how much money is really available in your account for future cheques or withdrawals? Also, there is greater potential for NSF cheques if you don't take the time necessary to reconcile.

Let's practice. Grab your last chequing statement or passbook. You will also need your cheque register where you recorded all your transactions as they happened. Some people like to use duplicate cheques as their cheque register, but there is more than just cheques going through your account, so the use of a cheque register is suggested. You have to consider all withdrawals made, EDM's, bill payments made over the phone, mortgage payments, loan payments, interest income and service charges, just to name a few. If anyone else has access to your account, like your spouse, they must give you records of all transactions they did on the account to give you an accurate picture. Reconciliation means you are performing a check and balance of your account to make sure everything is accounted for. From my experience, I would say that with married couples, over 90% of the time it is the wife who reconciles the accounts. If this is the case in your household, then husbands be patient, understanding and provide for your wife a record of everything you do on the account, because even though she is doing the reconciling, you were involved in the actual transactions that took place on the account. Also, you don't have to be an accountant or have bookkeeping experience to do this.

Please follow these instructions:

1. Tick or mark each matching item (both deposits and withdrawals or credits and debits) as they appear on both your

31

cheque register and the statement/passbook until each item on the statement/passbook is accounted for.

Cheque Register Example:

Cheque#	Date	Description of Cheque or Deposit	Amount	Balance
		Balance Carried Forward		$325.67
101	08/22/96	Groceries	$101.20	-$101.20
		Balance Carried Forward		$224.47
	08/22/96	Withdrawal from Bank Machine	$20.00	-$20.00
		Balance Carried Forward		$204.47
	08/22/96	Bill Payment – Hydro	$67.94	-$67.94
		Balance Carried Forward		$136.53
	08/22/96	Barry's Paycheque	$1,037.80	$1,037.80
		Balance Carried Forward		$1,174.33

2. In your cheque register, record any interest earned or service charges paid and tick these off on both your cheque register and the statement/passbook.

3. Now let's turn our attention to the worksheet provided on p. 34.

4. Find the last balance recorded on your statement/passbook and put this number beside "Last Balance (A)." In the example below, your number would be $849.66.

From Statement or Passbook:

Date	Description	Amount (+/-)	Balance
08/30/96	Cheque 105	$152.39	$859.54
08/31/96	Interest Earned	$0.42	$859.96
	Monthly Service Charge	$10.30	$849.66
(this is the end of the statement/passbook time frame)			

5. Itemize each deposit, ECM (Electronic Credit Memo) or credit which does not appear on this statement/passbook but does appear in your cheque register. Add these together to get (B). Subtotal (A) plus (B) to equal (C).

6. Now itemize and list all withdrawals, EDM's or debits which do not appear on your statement/passbook but do appear in your cheque register. Add these together to get (D).

32

7. Next you want to take (C) and subtract (D) from it to give you (E).

8. Hopefully, you will recognize the number that appears in (E) because it should match with the last total you have in your cheque register. If it doesn't, then something is out of balance and you should double check your entries.

NOTE:

For this to work properly, you must start with a balance you know to be an accurate balance of your account. Otherwise, the (E) above may not match the balance you show in your cheque register. If it isn't accurate, then the only way to correct it is to go back into previous months or to use a little trial and error to get yourself balanced. Once you know you have a balanced number to start with, don't lose it because all the months ahead will depend on your accuracy of this number.

If you have a home PC, there is software available to assist you with this task of bank reconciliation which you may want to research if you enjoy computers. These programs also help you with other areas of personal finance, including budgeting, analysis and forecasting.

Chequing Account Reconciliation for the Time Frame of: _____			
Last Balance	$_____	(A)	
Itemize each Credit/Deposit/ECM, etc.:			
*	$		
*	$		
*	$		
*	$		
*	$		
*	$		
*	$		
*	$_____		
Subtotal: $	$_____	(B)	
Add (A) plus (B) to get (C):	$	(C)	
Itemize each Debit/Withdrawal/EDM, etc.:			
*	$		
*	$		
*	$		
*	$		
*	$		
*	$		
*	$		
*	$		
*	$		
*	$		
*	$		
*	$		
*	$		
*	$_____		
Subtotal: $	$_____	(D)	
Take (C) and subtract (D) to get (E):	$	(E)	

Compare (E) to your cheque register balance.

Budgeting – The Basics

$ $ $

Most financial counselors will tell you that the main reason people suffer needless financial hardship is often because they don't budget their income, expenses and savings on a consistent basis. Many individuals and families don't have the knowledge necessary to prepare a realistic budget. Often they don't have the willpower or discipline to keep themselves within their budget even if they have the knowledge.

We live in a society where needs and wants often get confused. They tend to overlap in a large grey zone. No matter how we try to resist the temptation to spend, our senses and emotions convince us that we need that item now without a moment's more thought. Impulse spending will defeat any budget unless you have enough excess money in your budget to allocate as "impulse spending." Take the time needed to stand back from the temptation to impulse spend and really evaluate whether you need the product or service. Seek advice from others if necessary. If it is the last one of its kind available and the salesperson is pressuring you to decide now, simply smile and say you need time to think about it and if someone else purchases it before you, then so be it. For some, this will be difficult to master.

Take the time to think through all purchases great or small. You may think that this statement is ridiculous. If you are purchasing a large ticket item, then sure, take the time to think it through (even though in less than an hour many of us are in the business manager's office signing documents for that new car). But all purchases, even if they are small in value? Next time you go grocery shopping, watch and listen to other shoppers. Many of them are reading jars to get the best ingredients for the best price – just like you are without knowing it. Many are comparing one spaghetti sauce with another to determine if the extra twenty-five cents is really worth what is inside the jar. These are small items. They are also important since food is necessary for survival. There will always be certain purchases you will not change from one paycheque to the next. I enjoy a certain cola whereas you may enjoy a certain brand of coffee. Just be careful what you spend your money on according to your budget for that item.

WHAT IS A BUDGET?

It is a method where your income is offset by all your expenses and savings. Savings is not usually classified as an "expense"; however, in a budget it is one area where your income is designated to be put aside. In a budget, you cannot spend or save more than what is your total income. In other words:

Total Income = Total Expenses + Total Savings

HOW DO YOU PREPARE A BUDGET?

We must first decide what items you will have in your budget that will represent the various income, expense and savings items. In pencil, put a tick or check mark beside the items below which relate to you and your household. The following is not inclusive, as you may have a certain income or expense item that I have not mentioned. Notice that some items such as utilities can be grouped together or separated out – it is up to you how you want to personalize your budget. As time goes on, you may have to add items or take items away, such as adding the expense of sending your children to a Christian school while taking the expense of daycare away.

Income Items:

- Your paycheque (use only the net take-home pay income here, after all deductions)

- Spouse's paycheque (use only the net take-home pay income here, after all deductions)

- Interest, dividend or investment income

- Federal or Provincial Child Tax Credit

- GST Rebate (happens on a quarterly basis)

- Pension income

- CPP benefit or OAS income

- Annuity or RRIF income, if retired

- Estate, Royalty or Rental income

- Money received from returning pop cans and bottles

- You may have other income items not listed

Expense Items:

- Tithe

- Food

- Household goods such as toilet paper, paper towels, soap, etc.

- Utilities (hydro, telephone, natural gas, heating oil, garbage disposal)

- Clothing (this can be subdivided further into individuals or left as a group)

- Vehicle gasoline

- Car Insurance

- Car maintenance

- Christmas, Birthday or other gifts

- Daycare, Tuition or Clubs

- Swimming, Ballet, or Piano Lessons, etc.

- Entertainment

- Special Family Night

- Mortgage, Loan, Line of Credit or Credit Card Payments

- Property Taxes, Fire Insurance

- Rent

- Bank Service Charges

- You may have other expense items not listed, like a Buffer Amount

Savings Items:

- Your RRSP

- Spouse's RRSP

- Vacation

- Saving for a special purchase like a home, computer or mountain bike

- Children's post-secondary education

- You may have other savings items not listed

Once you have decided what your various items are for each of the three categories, you need to transpose these to your budget worksheet. You will find a blank budget worksheet at the end of this chapter on page 41 for you to fill in. For the time being, you only need to be concerned with the left hand side of the worksheet. Start filling in the item names on the worksheet. You will also find a completed budget worksheet on page 42 to show you what the final outcome will look like.

NUMBER CRUNCHING

Sharpen your pencil and dust off your calculator. I have come to appreciate that some people are not "number" people, and those people may find this next section a challenge. However, I think it will be well worth the effort you put into it. When finished, you will and should be proud of your accomplishment. Whether a "number" person or not, read the following instructions and patiently follow along.

I find it easiest to keep track of a budget on a per pay period basis. However, every individual or household is different; for instance, in a two income family, one spouse may be paid this week while the other is paid the next week. For your budget, figure out what works best for you and stay with it.

Pull out the budget worksheet you have just completed with the items listed on the left hand side. In the "Income Items" section, fill in the dollar figure for each of the items listed and add them together beside "Total Income." As stated above, use only the net pay after Federal Tax, CPP, UIC and other deductions are taken off. This is the actual disposable income you have to spend and save, therefore, it is the number we will use in your budget.

Next, let's look at your Expense Items under the "Budget" heading. You have to be reasonable and weigh what is more important to you than another item in your expense list and how much you are going to budget for that item. There are many fixed expense items such as rent, mortgage payment, loan payment, etc. Fill those in first since they are the easiest. If you are married, you should consider doing this as a couple, since you will both appreciate all the trade-offs and compromises you are going to encounter. I can't give you a lot of advice here except take your time and remember that there will be some give and take here. Remember the equation of:

Total Income = Total Expenses + Total Savings

I bring this equation to your attention here because, while making sure your expenses don't add up to more than your total income, you must remember the "Savings Items" section. Input your budget amounts for the savings items listed also at this time.

To help you keep track of this equation, in the bottom right hand corner of the worksheet is a "Summary" section. Input your totals for each of the three sections in their appropriate place and see what your end result becomes. You would like this to be $0 or a positive number. If it becomes a negative number, you have to go back and shave off your expenses or savings enough to get this end result to $0 or a slight positive. On page 42, you will find a worksheet that gives an example of what a completed budget looks like. Once you have accomplished this, then read on because now you get to see how the practical side of this exercise works in real life.

For some items in both the expense and savings sections of your budget, you should consider setting up a separate account. An example would be putting money away in an account for your property taxes or car insurance, plus having another account for your savings items such as vacation or special purchases. You should check into what service charges there would be to maintain each of these additional accounts. Many FI's have methods of automatically transferring specific amounts of money from your main general account to these other accounts (again check the service charges). Your RSP savings should definitely be set up as an automatic debit, or withdrawal from your account. More about the RSP's in a later chapter.

COMMITMENT CORNER

Look at the top right hand corner of your budget. Use this place to make a promise to both yourself and the others in your household. Use it for others in your household to make a promise back to you also. You are promising to stick to your budget. This way all of you will think twice before you impulse purchase. It also shows how important a balanced budget means to you. You can each initial or sign as your pledge. Use whatever method of commitment works best for you and your household to show accountability. Remember to pray about your budget and your commitment to it. We each need God's strength and guidance in all we do, including our personal finances.

As mentioned earlier in this book, there are computer programs available that help you in budgeting. You can also create your own spreadsheet if you have the correct software. How a budget is pulled together needs to be understood first before you purchase any special software or create your own spreadsheet. That is what this chapter and the next chapter on budgeting are all about – the basics and the practical application.

BUDGET WORKSHEET

Budget for the Pay Period of: _____					
Income Items:			**Commitment Corner:**		
	$				
	$				
	$				
	$				
Total Income	$				
Expense Items:	**Budget**	**Actual**	**Running Tally:**		
	$	$	**Expense Item:**		
	$	$		$	$
	$	$		$	$
	$	$		$	$
	$	$		$	$
	$	$	**On-going Total**	$	$
	$	$			
	$	$	**Expense Item:**		
	$	$		$	$
	$	$		$	$
	$	$		$	$
	$	$		$	$
	$	$	**On-going Total**	$	$
	$	$			
	$	$	**Expense Item:**		
	$	$		$	$
	$	$		$	$
	$	$		$	$
	$	$		$	$
Total Expenses	$	$	**On-going Total**	$	$
Savings Items:	**Budget**	**Actual**			
	$	$	**Summary**	**Budget**	**Actual**
	$	$	Total Income=	$	$
	$	$	Total Expenses=	$	$
	$	$	Total Savings=	$	$
	$	$	End Result (+/-)	$	$
Total Savings	$	$			

BUDGET COMPLETE

Budget for the Pay Period of: August 18-31						
Income Items:			**Commitment Corner:**			
Bob's Paycheque	$ 1,037.82					
Kay's Paycheque	$ 863.67					
Fed Child Tax Cr.	$ 35.00					
Interest Income	$ 3.11					
Total Income	$ 1,939.60					
Expense Items:	**Budget**	**Actual**	**Running Tally:**			
Tithe	$ 240.00	$	**Expense Item:**			
Food	$ 275.00	$			$	$
Household Goods	$ 45.00	$			$	$
Hydro	$ 40.00	$			$	$
Telephone	$ 15.00	$			$	$
Adult Clothing	$ 55.00	$	**On-going Total**		$	$
Kid's Clothing	$ 55.00	$				
Vehicle Gasoline	$ 55.00	$	**Expense Item:**			
Car Insurance	$ 100.00	$			$	$
Car Maintenance	$ 30.00	$			$	$
Christmas Gifts	$ 20.00	$			$	$
Swimming Lessons	$ 10.00	$			$	$
Children's Clubs	$ 5.00	$			$	$
Entertainment	$ 50.00	$	**On-going Total**		$	$
Family Night	$ 40.00	$				
Bank Charges	$ 10.30	$	**Expense Item:**			
Mortgage Payment	$ 423.58	$			$	$
Loan Payment	$ 180.00	$			$	$
Property Taxes	$ 80.00	$			$	$
Buffer Amount	$ 0.00	$			$	$
Total Expenses	$ 1,728.88	$ 0.00	**On-going Total**		$	$
Savings Items:	**Budget**	**Actual**				
Bob's RRSP	$ 50.00	$	**Summary**	**Budget**	**Actual**	
Kay's RRSP	$ 50.00	$	**Total Income=**	$1,939.60	$ 0.00	
Vacation	$ 60.00	$	**Total Expenses=**	$1,728.88	$ 0.00	
Special Purchase	$ 50.00	$	**Total Savings=**	$ 210.00	$ 0.00	
			End Result (+/-)	$ 0.72	$ 0.00	
Total Savings	$ 210.00	$ 0.00				

Budgeting – Practical
Application

$ $ $

Your budget has been fine-tuned and miraculously you have it balanced. You are now committed to your budget. Be pleased with yourself because most governments are unable to balance their budgets. Instead, they continue to go further into debt, putting added financial burdens on us and future generations. Similarly, if you don't start with a balanced budget, you could be faced with added financial burdens in the future. However, the practical application in real life will reveal if you truly balanced your budget.

Pull out your budget sheet again and you will see the headings "Actual." In the application of a budget, you need to keep accurate records of how much money is spent on each item for the time frame chosen. When the time frame is complete, add up your totals and complete the summary section to see if you balanced.

Keep yourself organized. You will want to see all receipts for all purchases. If a receipt is not available, then you must record the amount of the expenditure before you forget. You may want to keep these receipts for future reference so a filing system might be needed. In a previous chapter, we discussed reconciling your bank statement. This is also important since without a reconciled bank statement you will have trouble keeping accurate records of where your money went. Develop your own organized method of keeping receipts and records accurately.

Now, the time has come to fill in the "Actual." To the right hand side of the worksheet, you will find a section called "Running Tally." This is split into six sections. There are items in our budget expense side which don't have one or two easy entries, such as buying groceries or purchasing gasoline for our car(s); we do this more than once per paycheque. The Running Tally lets you keep an on-going total of these items. Choose the expense items that will have more than one entry and use the Running Tally. Have a look at a finished worksheet at the end of this chapter and that will give you all the explanation you need.

The time has come to fill in the "Actual." Again, remember your commitment and pray daily about your budget.

From this point on, I am presuming your first real life actual budget is complete. You may have found it difficult, but let me encourage you that the first time we do almost anything new it seems strange to us. But as we gain experience and learn from the past, it can become enjoyable (or at least bearable for some). Your final actual "Summary" numbers are complete. Now is the time to evaluate what was correct and what needs attention.

At the end of this chapter are two complete budget worksheet examples. One is called OVER BUDGET and the other is BALANCED BUDGET. If you are over budget, it means you spent more money than actually came in. Look at each item in your budget expense and savings to see where modifications can be made. According to our equation of **Total Income = Total Expense + Total Savings**, you have two choices to get your budget balanced in the future. Either earn more money (which is not that simple) to increase the Total Income side, or decrease the amount of Total Expense or Total Savings. Usually, you have more control over decreasing Total Expense or Total Savings. May I suggest you concentrate on lowering the Total Expense more than the Total Savings? Your savings are for financial security in the future and if you have developed the habit of saving consistently, then to stop this could jeopardize your ability to get back into the savings habit again. Only if nothing else can be done to the expense side should you look at lowering your savings side.

Do not give up because you are over budget. For the future's sake, take the time to evaluate the past in order to plan and prepare for the future. Learn from the experience as you prepare your next budget. Also, continue to pray for God's direction and wisdom in your personal finances.

If you are under budget, you are in the minority. I suggest you put the excess into your savings section or use the extra that God has given you to help others in need and receive God's blessing for doing so. Read Matthew 6: 1-4.

If your budget is balanced, be pleased with your efforts and congratulate each other (without spending money, of course, unless it is budgeted for!) and make sure you thank God also.

Sometimes the difficulty in budgeting is that before the previous budget time frame has been completed and evaluated, you are starting to prepare your next budget worksheet. After you have done a few of these, you will be able to evaluate quickly whatever needs to be done in your budget in order to balance it both before and after the actual is complete.

May God bless your efforts in budgeting. Pray for your own budgeting as well as for other Christians who are seeking God's direction in their personal finances. We need to be both good stewards of all that God has provided and accountable to Him and each other.

Over Budget

Budget for the Pay Period of: August 18-31

Income Items:

Income Items:		Commitment Corner:
Bob's Paycheque	$ 1,037.82	
Kay's Paycheque	$ 863.67	
Fed Child Tax Cr.	$ 35.00	
Interest Income	$ 3.11	
Total Income	**$ 1,939.60**	

Expense Items:	Budget	Actual	Running Tally:		
Tithe	$ 240.00	$ 240.00	**Expense Item:**	**Food**	**Gasoline**
Food	$ 275.00	$ 289.25		$ 185.26	$ 22.00
Household Goods	$ 45.00	$ 32.00		$ 4.77	$ 18.00
Hydro	$ 40.00	$ 38.00		$ 85.24	$ 12.00
Telephone	$ 15.00	$ 18.00		$ 13.98	$
Adult Clothing	$ 55.00	$ 60.00	**On-going Total**	$ 289.25	$ 52.00
Kid's Clothing	$ 55.00	$ 52.00			
Vehicle Gasoline	$ 55.00	$ 57.00	**Expense Item:**	**Entertain**	
Car Insurance	$ 100.00	$ 100.00		$ 17.56	$
Car Maintenance	$ 30.00	$ 84.88		$ 12.68	$
Christmas Gifts	$ 20.00	$ 20.00		$ 5.70	$
Children's Clubs	$ 5.00	$ 10.00		$ 48.94	$
Swimming Lessons	$ 10.00	$ 10.00		$	$
Entertainment	$ 50.00	$ 30.00	**On-going Total**	$ 84.88	$
Family Night	$ 40.00	$ 38.50			
Bank Charges	$ 10.30	$ 15.50	**Expense Item:**		
Mortgage Payment	$ 423.58	$ 423.58		$	$
Loan Payment	$ 180.00	$ 215.00		$	$
Property Taxes	$ 80.00	$ 80.00		$	$
Buffer Amount	$ 0.00	$ 0.00		$	$
Total Expenses	**$ 1,728.88**	**$ 1,813.71**	**On-going Total**	$	$

Savings Items:	Budget	Actual			
Bob's RRSP	$ 50.00	$ 50.00	**Summary**	**Budget**	**Actual**
Kay's RRSP	$ 50.00	$ 50.00	**Total Income=**	$1,939.60	$1,939.60
Vacation	$ 60.00	$ 60.00	**Total Expenses=**	$1,728.88	$1,813.71
Special Purchase	$ 50.00	$ 50.00	**Total Savings=**	$ 210.00	$ 210.00
			End Result (+/-)	$ 0.72	$ -84.11
Total Savings	**$ 210.00**	**$ 210.00**			

Balanced Budget

Budget for the Pay Period of: August 18-31					
Income Items:			**Commitment Corner:**		
Bob's Paycheque	$ 1,037.82				
Kay's Paycheque	$ 863.67				
Fed Child Tax Cr.	$ 35.00				
Interest Income	$ 3.11				
Total Income	$ 1,939.60				
Expense Items:	**Budget**	**Actual**	**Running Tally:**		
Tithe	$ 240.00	$ 240.00	**Expense Item:**	**Food**	**Gasoline**
Food	$ 275.00	$ 289.25		$ 185.26	$ 22.00
Household Goods	$ 45.00	$ 25.00		$ 4.77	$ 18.00
Hydro	$ 40.00	$ 38.00		$ 85.24	$ 12.00
Telephone	$ 15.00	$ 18.00		$ 13.98	$
Adult Clothing	$ 55.00	$ 30.00	**On-going Total**	$ 289.25	$ 52.00
Kid's Clothing	$ 55.00	$ 52.00			
Vehicle Gasoline	$ 55.00	$ 52.00	**Expense Item:**	**Entertain**	
Car Insurance	$ 100.00	$ 100.00		$ 17.56	$
Car Maintenance	$ 30.00	$ 38.00		$ 12.68	$
Christmas Gifts	$ 20.00	$ 20.00		$ 5.70	$
Children's Clubs	$ 5.00	$ 5.00		$	$
Swimming Lessons	$ 10.00	$ 10.00		$	$
Entertainment	$ 50.00	$ 35.94	**On-going Total**	$ 35.94	$
Family Night	$ 40.00	$ 36.50			
Bank Charges	$ 10.30	$ 9.70	**Expense Item:**		
Mortgage Payment	$ 423.58	$ 423.58		$	$
Loan Payment	$ 180.00	$ 215.00		$	$
Property Taxes	$ 80.00	$ 80.00		$	$
Buffer Amount	$ 0.00	$ 0.00		$	$
Total Expenses	$ 1,728.88	$1,717.97	**On-going Total**	$	$
Savings Items:	**Budget**	**Actual**			
Bob's RRSP	$ 50.00	$ 50.00	**Summary**	**Budget**	**Actual**
Kay's RRSP	$ 50.00	$ 50.00	**Total Income=**	$1,939.60	$1,939.60
Vacation	$ 60.00	$ 60.00	**Total Expenses=**	$1,728.88	$1,717.97
Special Purchase	$ 50.00	$ 50.00	**Total Savings=**	$ 210.00	$ 210.00
			End Result (+/-)	$ 0.72	$ 11.63
Total Savings	$ 210.00	$ 210.00			

Summary of Day-To-Day Personal Finances

$ $ $

- Look into what types of bank accounts you have and whether there is a service package available that could save you money on your service charges.

- Inquire at your Bank, Trust or Credit Union about Deposit Insurance.

- If you need an overdraft facility, make sure it is only for a reasonable amount. If necessary, check into other debt instruments to see if they are cheaper on the interest rate.

- Your bank card provides convenience banking. It will also have other uses in the years to come.

- Economists provide useful information, but be careful how you apply what they say to your personal finances. Do your own research in light of their opinions.

- For security, you may consider a Safe Deposit Box to store your valuables. Ensure that you review the types of registration allowed and set your box up for what is best for you.

- You need to know where you have been in order to know where you are going. That is why reconciling your chequing account regularly is a good idea. Use the worksheet provided as a guide.

- Sometimes it feels like our paycheques are gone before the next pay day and we don't have a clue as to where it was spent. That is why you need a budget. If you are married, work together patiently on this. As with all aspects of our lives, always pray about your personal finances.

- Use the budget worksheet provided as a guide to help you in balancing where your money is going and why it is going there. This will be time well spent.

SECTION TWO

Investments

$ $ $

Topics covered in this section will help you in managing and making decisions about your investments inside or outside of an RRSP.

"Do not store up for yourselves treasures on earth, where moth and rust destroy, and where thieves break in and steal. But store up for yourselves treasures in heaven, where moth and rust do not destroy, and where thieves do not break in and steal. For where your treasure is, there your heart will be also. The eye is the lamp of the body. If your eyes are good, your whole body will be full of light. But if your eyes are bad, your whole body will be full of darkness. If then the light within you is darkness, how great is that darkness! No one can serve two masters. Either he will hate the one and love the other, or he will be devoted to the one and despise the other. You cannot serve both God and Money."

Matthew 6:19-24

But godliness with contentment is great gain. For we brought nothing into the world, and we can take nothing out of it. But if we have food and clothing, we will be content with that. People who want to get rich fall into temptation and a trap and into many foolish and harmful desires that plunge men into ruin and destruction. For the love of money is a root of all kinds of evil. Some people, eager for money, have wandered from the faith and pierced themselves with many griefs.

1 Timothy 6:6-10

The Investor & the Investments

$ $ $

The Bible doesn't say we are not to invest our money, but we are to make sure our motives for saving money are correct with God. In Canada, there are quite a few investment opportunities available. However, you will hear that our country represents only a small portion of all the investment opportunities available around the world. We need to understand the investment types available before we start investing either in Canada or globally.

Countries go through a business or economic cycle of recession to recovery. The cycle can vary in time frame. Recession is an extended drop in economic activity. Governments attempt to get their economies into the recovery state by dropping interest rates to stimulate consumer spending due to cheaper borrowing costs. This contracts the spending power of most senior citizens who have a majority of their investments tied into interest-sensitive products, which means that they rely on higher interest rates to provide them with greater income. Often other factors hinder this reduction in interest rates such as inflation, government policies, global trading restrictions or even oil import prices (remember the late '70s and early '80s). Another factor is consumer confidence. You may have the lower interest rates and everything else appears to be in the government's favour, but if consumers are concerned about the stability of their jobs, it will be difficult to get them to open their wallets and spend their disposable income. There is a considerable number of individuals and families that are heavily into debt and don't have either the extra borrowing power or the available disposable income to spend more to stimulate the economy. Therefore, a lot of factors go into an economy's cycle of contraction (recession) and expansion (recovery or growth).

Below you will find a graph that compares investment types on their return potential compared to the possible risk you will have to take to receive that return. This is not an all inclusive listing of investment opportunities. Note that the higher the risk, the potentially higher the return over the long term. However, also note that the higher the risk, the greater the potential for large losses over the short or long term.

SAVINGS ACCOUNT

Your savings account doesn't pay you a lot of interest because this money is available upon your demand for it. This is why, in the banking industry, we call this money "demand savings." Depending on whether you are over your deposit insurance limitations as per an earlier chapter, this money provides you with the lowest risk for investment purposes. However, most investors only carry what is needed for day-to-day living in their savings or chequing accounts.

CANADA SAVINGS BONDS

Every fall the Federal Government issues another series in their Canada Savings Bonds. When you purchase one of these bonds, you are lending the government your money for a specified rate of return. They pay better interest than a savings account and they come in low denominations (as low as $100.00), so you don't have to have a lot of money available to invest in a CSB.

Currently, these bonds have a maturity of 10-12 years depending on which CSB's you have, and they usually come with some sort of interest rate guarantee for a specific time frame. In other words, the CSB may come with a guarantee of 8% minimum interest rate in its first year, 7% minimum interest rate for the second year and 6% for the third, etc. That is the minimum guaranteed. You may find that when the second year arrives, the CSB will guarantee 8% again, but it will not go lower than the 7% promised during that second year. Or, if the interest rate announced for the new series is 6%, you would receive the 7% promised to you the previous year since the promise was that the second year would not pay less than 7%. With each annual CSB issue, the Federal Government prints an easy-to-read pamphlet which explains previous CSB issues and the current CSB offered. If interested, request a copy from your FI.

Another reason investors like the CSB is because they can be cashed easily at their FI. There are a couple of items to remember here, however. When you purchase a CSB, it starts paying you interest immediately; however, if you cash it in within the first 60 days from November 1st (usually it is this date), you will not receive any interest on the CSB, but will receive only the full face value. Also, if you need to cash in a CSB, do so on the first day of the month. This way you will receive all the interest owing to you for the previous month.

Example:

> *On July 13th you decide to cash in your CSB. If you proceed with this transaction on July 13th, then you will only be paid interest up to and including June 30th, not up to the 13th of July. If you wait until August 1st to cash in the CSB, then you will receive the full month's interest of July and not miss out on any interest income.*

The Federal Government wants to have its debt load funded as much as possible by Canadians instead of foreign investors. Sales of CSB's have been going down over the past few years. This will not be acceptable to the government so you will probably see more creative methods of making CSB's or similar investment instruments available to Canadians. One possibility is to offer CSB's not just in the fall of each year, but maybe year round. CSB's are already being sold as an RRSP (Registered Retirement Savings Plan) investment alternative in order for the government to tap into this market to raise funds to support its debt load.

There are also Provincial Savings Bonds available. Often these will try to pay higher rates of return than your FI or the CSB's in order to attract investors. Just remember that on a risk scale, the provincial bonds are a higher risk because it is the Federal Government that transfers large sums of money to the provinces, so the Federal Government is more in control of a province's finances than the province itself. When you hear in the news discussions about "transfer payments to the provinces," this is to what I am referring.

MUTUAL FUNDS

You will find a couple of chapters in this book devoted to Mutual Funds. Therefore, from the graph on the previous page note where each type of mutual fund fits in with risk and returns. Detailed discussion will come later.

TREASURY BILLS

These are also called Money Market instruments. They are issued by the Federal Government to raise short term funds, which means they are issued for a year or less in duration. The most famous is the 91-day T-Bill. You should note that T-Bills don't pay you interest like other investments. Instead, they are sold at a discount which means they will return a yield to the investor.

Example:

Instead of buying a $10,000.00 T-Bill for 91 days, you would purchase a $9,900.00 T-Bill which will mature in 91 days at a value of $10,000.00. To calculate yield, you do the following:

Interest Earned x 365 ÷ # Days in T-Bills = Yield (%)
Purchase Amount

$$\frac{\$100.00}{\$9900.00} \times \frac{365}{91} = 4.0\%$$

GUARANTEED INVESTMENT CERTIFICATES

A similar product is also called Term Deposits. These are sold by FI's and will guarantee a specific rate of return for a specific time frame. Usually, you cannot cash these in early unless the certificate allows this in its terms and conditions. Instead, the FI will allow you to borrow against the GIC if you need the funds, but usually at a higher rate of interest than what you are receiving on the GIC. Since you are locking in your funds for a specified time frame, the FI will give you a better rate of return than if you left the money in your savings account.

BONDS

There are various types of bonds available which include Federal Government Bonds, Provincial Government Bonds, Corporate Bonds and Municipal Bonds. These are not to be confused with Canada Savings Bonds. There are bond rating agencies that research the governments or companies and put a rating on the debt of each. The better the rating, usually the lower the rate of return the bond issuer will have to promise when issuing his bond in the marketplace because there is a perceived lower risk with that bond. Take note that not all provincial bonds are rated equally. Each province will be rated individually. Therefore, a bond issued by British Columbia could be rated differently than one from Newfoundland due to the risk the bond rating agency places on each province. The same goes for corporate and municipal bonds. This information is often available at the larger public libraries, through a stock broker or by various other publications.

If you are going to purchase individual bonds, make sure you do your research first as to the bond rating, but also be aware of both what the feature of the bond is and how a bond works in relation to the bond market as a whole. There are bonds that are convertible to shares or stock, that are redeemable, extendible or retractable, or that have other features. Be knowledgeable of what features come with a bond before purchasing it as an investment.

Generally speaking, this is how a bond works. It is separated into two potential ways of making you a return. The first is the interest rate or yield. If the bond is issued at 8% interest rate, you will be paid that rate of return by the bond issuer at the bond's maturity. The second way is marketability of the bond on the bond market. This comes into play especially if you have to sell your bond early before maturity. You can buy or sell your bond on the bond market just as you can buy or sell stocks on the stock market. However, you may find the $5,000.00 bond you purchased is now worth $5,100.00 on the bond market, or the opposite, $4,800.00. Why is this when the face value of the bond and the amount you paid for the bond was $5,000.00?

Example of "premium selling":

You buy a bond with a guaranteed rate of return of 10%. The economy is in a bit of a contraction now and the government is trying to stimulate the economy by lowering interest rates. Currently, a similar bond is giving a rate of return of 8%. You are pleased because you are being paid 10%. Another investor approaches you and offers to buy your 10% bond from you. You know he can only get 8% in the marketplace so you agree to sell it to him but only if he pays you a "premium" for the ability to obtain that 10% rate of return. He agrees since he wants the higher rate of return and the premium charged is not unrealistic or it doesn't cut too heavily into the gains he will make on the higher rate of return bond. You have received the 10% rate of return all along and now you made a further bonus on the sale of your bond due to the direction of interest rates.

Example of "discount selling":

The opposite is also true. You have the 10% bond, but now interest rates are at 12%. If you don't need to sell the bond, then fine because you will still receive the 10% rate of return and at maturity of the bond you will receive the face value dollar for dollar. However, if you need to sell the bond before maturity and interest rates are at 12% for a similar bond, then to find a buyer you will have to sell at a discount in order to attract an investor to accept the lower interest rate than what the markets are giving. This is a loss to you because you will receive less than face value for that bond. Therefore, be careful and know what you are doing when buying bonds as an investment.

To compare bond yields, the following equation can be used:

$$\text{Current Yield} = \frac{\text{Annual Interest in Dollars}}{\text{Current Market Price of the Bond}}$$

Example:

Current Yield = $\dfrac{5\% \times \$5,000.00}{\$4,500.00}$ (Face Value of Bond) (Current Price of Bond) = 5.55%

Current Yield = $\dfrac{5\% \times \$5,000.00}{\$5,500.00}$ (Face Value of Bond) (Current Price of Bond) = 4.55%

If you are trying to calculate Yield to Maturity (YTM), this equation is much more difficult to calculate and I would refer you to your financial advisor or broker for this information.

STOCKS AND SHARES

A Preferred Share gets its name from the fact that if a company fails, then the preferred share holders will get paid before the common share holders. Preferred shares can come with other options also, such as a convertibility to a specific number of common shares or variable rate, cumulative or non-cumulative, plus other features. Preferred shares are often more difficult to purchase as they are sometimes not as available on the markets for sale by investors. There aren't as many preferred shares issued as common shares. You may have certain rights that relate to the company since you are now a part owner of the company by being a shareholder. If a company was to dissolve or liquidate, then the preferred shareholders have more risk than the bond holders, but less risk than the common shareholders because the bond holders will be paid first from the remaining company assets, then the preferred shareholders and then the common shareholders.

Common Shares are usually readily available on the stock markets. There are instances when publicly traded common shares aren't available for sale for certain companies, but this is very rare. You are usually paid a dividend at a specified time. I say "usually" as the dividend is determined by company earnings and availability of funds to pay out dividends. Other possible income is from share value appreciation. This means that if the share price goes up, then your shares are worth more money if you were to sell them. However, the opposite is also very true. You may be receiving the dividend, but the share value has gone down. If you sell, you would be taking a loss. You may want to hold the investment and weather the storm and see what happens in the long term. This will depend on your investment strategy. You are an owner or stakeholder in the company, so you will have certain rights available to you such as voting at general meetings for election of directors, choosing the auditor or other matters.

OTHER INVESTMENTS

There are other investments from stamp and hockey card collections to real estate or gold to collecting coins and antiques. When getting into specialty investments, be careful because if you had to sell on short notice for whatever reason, you want to make sure there are readily available purchasers willing to pay your price.

Investor Strategy

$ $ $

When choosing your investment portfolio, there are possible risks involved and your personal investment style that you should consider before making any purchases.

MARKET TIMING RISK

This risk means that if you had to sell your investment due to an emergency or cash flow problem, you could be selling the investment at a poor time according to the markets. That stock you purchased for $10/share is now worth only $7/share; your bond is returning you 8%, but interest rates are currently at 11%; or that mutual fund was bought at $11.63/unit and currently you can only get $9.56/unit.

With investing, you want to buy low and sell high, not the other way around. However, circumstances may come into play sometimes.

INTEREST RATE RISK

In the "Bonds" section of the previous chapter, this was discussed. However, there is another risk for people who are on fixed incomes at retirement. If you are relying on the interest returns on your investments to provide for your retirement income, you run a risk of having to dip into the principal amount of your investment when interest rates are extremely low. There have been many people retiring with the expectation that interest rates would not go to record lows, only to see that their interest income is not supporting their standard of living as they had planned.

CASHABILITY RISK

Another word often used is liquidity. How easily can you cash in your investment on the marketplace? Will it sell immediately or will you have to wait until a buyer comes forward? In order to sell, will you have to take a loss? This is of greater concern when you get into specialty investments such as real estate, coins and stamps, etc.

CURRENCY RISK

If you are purchasing investments in a foreign currency, then that investment is valuated against the currency to which you either bought or will sell the investment. What is meant here is that if I purchase 100 shares of a Japanese stock with my Canadian dollars and then sell the shares and receive Canadian dollars, then I am concerned with how the Japanese yen compares to the Canadian dollar both when I purchased the shares and when I sold them. If for some reason the yen was high when I bought and low when I sold, then this could affect my actual return on my investment.

ADVICE RISK

If you use a stock broker, financial advisor or the advice of a friend when making your investment decisions, be sure that you are comfortable with both the person giving you the advice and the risk associated with that investment strategy or plan. Whoever you use for advice will not be correct 100% of the time, but you are looking for a genuine concern in that person for your personal financial needs and not simply their needs. There is a definite trust factor here. Hopefully, a Christian brother or sister would be a good choice, but you personally have to be very comfortable with the fact that whoever you choose for advice will know a lot about your personal finances and they must have your best interests in mind. Also, remember that if you choose a Christian advisor, they are not perfect. Know the person from whom you are receiving your advice.

INVESTMENT STYLE

It is important that you decide what style or type of investor you are. Note that for married couples, one spouse may be a certain investor type while the other is either more conservative or more risk-oriented. Remember that your investment choices affect the whole family unit in the future, therefore, consideration of the other spouse when investing should be given. Various factors should be considered including age, income, net worth, investment knowledge and experience and tolerance to risk to name a few.

Ultra-Conservative Approach

This style wants nothing to do with stocks or bonds, but will only invest in GIC's or CSB's for their investment portfolio. These investors are extremely risk adverse. They will consider the interest rate risk to be the highest risk they will take. I have one suggestion for this type of investor: Stagger your maturity dates for short term (1 year or less in duration), medium term (2-3 years) and long term (4-5 years). The reason for this is that you do not want all of your portfolio maturing at the same time when interest rates are low. By staggering your maturities, you will hopefully renew at various interest rates instead of all your investments maturing on the same day at the same interest rate. I have seen a lot of fixed income retirees put all their money in one lump sum and state, "Interest rates can't get much lower," only to find out a few months later when it matures that indeed interest rates can get lower. Meanwhile, if they had staggered their maturities originally, they may have now been receiving better income returns.

Conservative Approach

This investor will have a mixture of investments. The majority will be in the lower risk versus return section of the graph as shown in the previous chapter. They will invest in GIC's and bonds or similar types of mutual funds with a small amount of their portfolio in stocks, usually blue chip stocks which are of large corporations that have established track records.

63

Balanced Approach

A small percentage of this portfolio will be in GIC's with the remainder split evenly between bonds and equities (shares). Again, mutual funds can be substituted here, and this will be discussed in the next chapter. You will have to consider the individual bond or share risk since every bond or stock is not the same. As a balanced investor, you are willing to take some risk; however, you are usually tugged toward the conservative side of investing.

Growth Approach

This approach is not risk adverse. In other words, these investors accept risk when they make their investment decisions. However, they also accept that this risk is for the long term and that on the short term, the risk may appear to hurt them (if they were to sell their portfolio early). If you lie awake at night worrying about your finances, this is definitely not for you. If you are retired or approaching retirement, then be careful if you are growth-oriented. If the values of your portfolio went down dramatically and you had to take a loss, then you are taking a loss on funds that are to provide a comfortable retirement.

This approach will have minimal GIC's, if any. There will be a small amount of bonds. The majority of funds will be in the equities with foreign content playing an important role.

What Approach Am I?

Talk this over with your financial advisor if you have one. If not, many FI's have investment quizzes or analyses that you can personally complete free of charge to see which approach fits you best. Each will call their approach by a different name. I would suggest you discover your style of investing and follow it. Your neighbour or friend may be telling you about that great investment he made that made him lots of money. You may feel that you are missing out and decide to invest in it yourself, even if it goes against your investment style. Of course, by now your friend has sold the investment without telling you, and you are losing money because the investment is going downhill fast. Does your friend ever tell about the "tips" that bombed on him or does he only talk about the ones that were successful? Avoid speculative investing unless you are willing to completely accept the risk involved in this approach. Instead, stick to your plan as per your investment approach.

The Bears & the Bulls

$ $ $

When you read that title, you may be thinking of various sports teams. However, these two terms are used in the financial market-place quite a lot. If you read a financial newspaper, you may see the headline, "Bonds Are Very Bearish" or "The Stock Market is Continuing to Bull Ahead." What do these code words mean?

BEAR

A bear refers to when the markets are going down, or losing value. So if the stock market is in a "bear," then the stock market is going down. An individual stock may be talked about as being in a "bear." Different degrees of panic strike an investor when they hear the word "bear." You will see large volumes of trades on the stock markets when it is starting a bear because investors are trying to take their profits before the bear goes too deep downward. You will find economists divided as to when we are truly in a bear market, or if a "correction" is happening in the markets. The correction means that a bear appears to be happening, but it will rebound back into a bull shortly. However, they may not always be correct in their analysis. A very serious bear is a one-day market crash like we saw on Black Monday, October 19, 1987.

BULL

A bull is opposite to a bear. A bull market is when the markets are gaining or increasing in value. The unknown is how long the bull ride will last. When do you take your profits and be satisfied? Or, do you chance it further that the bull will continue? Decisions to make.

Market timing is how you make it or lose it sometimes. So, believe it or not, a bull market is a good thing. Right now, in the mid-1990s, investors have been enjoying a record-setting bull ride on the markets. Of course, what goes up must eventually come down.

These are very different terms, but as in any industry, there are often different terms used to describe different things relating to that industry.

Mutual Funds –
Questions & Answers

$ $ $

Mutual funds have been available to the public for many years, but in the 1980s, the general public took notice of them and have invested in them quite heavily ever since. Before entertaining mutual funds as part of your portfolio, you must first understand what investment style you are (previous chapter), then research the background information about mutual funds (this chapter) and finally, know what the difference is between the types of mutual funds available in the marketplace and through your FI (next chapter).

BACKGROUND INFORMATION ABOUT MUTUAL FUNDS

I am always asked lots of questions when it comes to mutual funds, so the following is a question and answer format to help you.

What Is a Mutual Fund?

A mutual fund is a pool of money from many investors like yourself that is used by a fund manager to purchase many securities on the behalf of you and the other investors. Since there are a wide range of mutual fund types available, there are many different opportunities for your investment dollars by way of a mutual fund without having to purchase and manage your own multi-million dollar portfolio, which most of us couldn't afford anyway.

Who Is This Fund Manager?

This could be an individual or a group of investment professionals, usually called an investment group or counsel, who specialize in the type of mutual fund for which they are responsible. If they are managers of bonds, then they won't be the fund manager of a special equity fund. They have specific disciplines of knowledge and experience in specific areas of the financial market.

Why Invest In a Mutual Fund?

Since there is a pool of money available to invest, the fund manager can diversify the funds into many different investments instead of just buying one or two stocks or bonds. Many of us simply don't have the money or time available to purchase a variety of investments. By investing in a mutual fund, you are reaping the benefits of diversification and, therefore, should make better returns for yourself over the long term.

Example:

If you had 100 shares of a particular stock, then all your money is in one investment. If that investment does well, then you are pleased. However, if that investment does poorly, you will question why you are holding it anymore. You are placing all your hope in that one investment. Whereas in a mutual fund, the fund manager may have chosen the exact same stock as you, but he also has other people's money available to him to purchase other stocks, etc., thus diversifying the risk over many different stocks instead of only one stock. Therefore, even if the stock you and the fund are holding goes down, there are other stocks that may or may not go down as well.

This is why on the graph on page 54 that compares risk and return, you will see the mutual fund as less risky than purchasing the stock or bond individually.

How Much Money Do I Need and How Often Do I Need To Invest In a Mutual Fund?

Some mutual funds have a minimum purchase amount as a requirement to invest in their mutual fund. Most mutual funds have no minimum amount if you set up a systematic plan where the mutual fund company will collect from your bank account a specific amount of money on a regular frequency (monthly, bi-weekly, etc.) to invest in the mutual fund(s) you have chosen. Every FI and mutual fund company will call this systematic plan by its own name, but they all do the same thing. Consider investing in a family of mutual funds on a systematic basis as it provides a forced savings plan. There may be special requirements when inside an RRSP that you should research, like foreign content.

Can I Hold Mutual Funds In My RRSP Plan?

The taxation rules currently state that you can hold mutual funds in your RRSP, RRIF (Registered Retirement Income Fund) and Self-Direct RRSP. However, you must keep within the "foreign content rule." This rule states that the maximum non-Canadian securities you can hold in your individual plan is 20% of that individual plan. This appears to be a little tricky and confusing because within the individual Canadian mutual funds, they too are allowed to have up to 20% foreign content within their mutual fund type. However, your 20% is not concerned with what is in the Canadian mutual fund, but only what individual mutual funds you have that are not Canadian content.

Example:

The following is acceptable:

Canadian Growth Fund you have as an investment in your RRSP has a maximum 20% of its value in foreign securities to take advantage of the foreign content rule. Do not be concerned with this as it does not affect your allowable 20% foreign content. You look at your RRSP plan and discover that you have a US Equity Mutual Fund and an International Equity Mutual Fund which add up to 20% of that particular plan value (all the mutual fund values in that family of mutual funds added together). This is fine as long as you don't purchase any more foreign content mutual funds and the income generated from these foreign content mutual funds doesn't put the total percentage over 20% of total plan value. Many mutual fund companies will monitor this for you on their computer systems and either sell the percentage that is above the 20% rule and place it in another Canadian mutual fund for you or notify you immediately. There is a penalty from Revenue Canada if you stay above the 20% allowable.

Why Is Foreign Content So Important In a Mutual Fund?

The Canadian financial markets make up a very small portion of the global markets. Therefore, to both spread your risk through diversification and to take advantage of the opportunities for good returns, foreign content should be considered as part of your portfolio. Many of us, however, do not have the expertise to invest globally with individual stocks or bonds. That is why a mutual fund that either specializes in foreign markets or has up to the 20% foreign content limit to be an eligible RRSP investment makes sense. This 20% rule is currently being reviewed by the Federal Government to see if it can be changed or maybe even eliminated. It was put in place originally to ensure that a market existed for Canadian securities. However, with the view towards "globalization," many investors would like to see this rule improved or eliminated altogether. When you look at the graph on page 54, you will see that the foreign content mutual funds are a higher risk, so make sure you do your homework on the mutual fund before you invest.

What Is Dollar-Cost-Averaging?

If you invest systematically on a regular basis, you are being very smart in your investment strategy. The value of a mutual fund will go up and down according to the market value of the investments held within the mutual fund. Therefore, the best time to invest, as we learned earlier, is when prices are low. However, market timing is often very difficult to accomplish successfully. By investing a specific dollar amount systematically, you will catch the highs and lows of your mutual fund value. Some mutual funds will actually show you the average cost of your investment in their quarterly or annual statement to you. If you do single lump sum purchases every year in your mutual fund, you will be accepting the fact that all of this money you are investing is going into the mutual fund on one specific day when the value of the mutual fund may or may not be low. You create an unnecessary risk to yourself by investing this way. As you can see, the best method is systematic regular purchases of your mutual fund to obtain the benefits of dollar-cost-averaging.

When values are down, you are actually purchasing more units of a fund which means that when the fund unit values go up, you will have more units at this higher price per unit.

Example:

Date	Purchase	Unit Value	# Units Purchased	Plan Value	Total # of Units Owned
Sept. 30	$25.00	11.63	2.15	$25.00	2.15
Oct. 30	$25.00	10.50	2.38	$47.57	4.53
Nov. 30	$25.00	12.72	1.97	$82.68	6.50
Totals:	**$75.00**	**12.72**	**6.50**	**$82.68**	**6.50**

Why Are Mutual Funds Called Units Instead of Shares?

A share is ownership of a particular company. A mutual fund may hold many shares of different companies and, therefore, the term "unit" is more appropriate since it isn't one share you own of one company. Whether the mutual fund type has shares or not, they are called units of that mutual fund type.

How Do You Determine What the Value of a Unit Is?

In the next chapter, you will learn what the various "types" of available mutual funds are. Basically, the value is determined by the market value of all the investments added together at the close of business each day divided by the number of outstanding units of that fund type. Usually, there aren't a maximum number of allowable units outstanding. There are a few closed mutual funds where they restrict the number of units, but these are rare. All Money Market Mutual Funds will have a unit value of $10.00. Their value will be shown as a particular yield, such as 5.36% annualized.

Can I Transfer Money Within the Mutual Fund Family?

The "mutual fund family" means that a mutual fund company may offer a variety of different mutual funds. Refer to the graph on page 54. The mutual fund family may have several, all or other mutual fund types. Each fund is its own entity, but it is under the umbrella or family of other mutual funds from the same company.

Many mutual fund companies will allow you to transfer funds from one fund type to another fund type without any extra charges. However, you should ask this question before you actually purchase a mutual fund so you know ahead of time. This information should also be found in the fund's Simplified Prospectus.

How Easy Is It To Get My Money Out of a Mutual Fund?

Usually it is quite easy, but there may be costs in taking the funds out according to the original contract you agreed to with the mutual fund company. Many mutual fund companies will take faxed or even verbal instructions over the phone. Also, if your mutual fund is in an RRSP, you could be faced with taxation implications.

What Is a Management Fee Expense?

This is a fee paid to the fund manager or investment counsel to pay their expenses and salaries. When you see the rates of return advertised for a mutual fund, the management fee expense has usually been taken off before the previous return is quoted. The management fee is taken as a percentage of the value of the fund type, such as 1.5%, etc. Each fund type will have a different percentage that goes towards management fees depending on the difficulty in managing that fund. You will see that Money Market funds are usually low in management fees and Global Mutual funds are much higher due to the amount of research, special knowledge and business costs required to manage this fund properly.

It is in the fund managers' best interests that the mutual fund type they are managing does very well because the higher the total value of the fund type at the time they are paid means the more they'll be paid since they are paid a percentage of the total plan value.

What Are the Charges or "Loads" I Will Pay to Purchase a Mutual Fund?

Every mutual fund is different here, so research and asking questions is a must. Some mutual funds will charge you to invest in their mutual fund. If you are going to invest with this company and are charged a fee, or load, then be aware that this could affect your rate of return on the mutual fund. Other mutual fund companies don't charge any load. There is a constant discussion as to whether a load or no-load fund is better for the investor. The load funds will say you pay for what you get and the no-load funds will say that all of your hard earned money is being invested instead of only a percentage. I would say that there are excellent load and no-load funds available and it is necessary to do your research to determine what is best for you.

Front-end load:

These can range from 1-9% but are usually around 5%. If you are charged a 5% front-end load on a $100.00 investment, then you are really investing only $95.00 since the other $5.00 is the load. Therefore, you must consider that the $5.00 is not being invested for you because it is no longer yours. The mutual fund company is investing the $95.00 for you and you will receive your return on the $95.00 investment only. Many times this load can be worth the advice you receive, but you must make that decision yourself.

Redemption or Back-End Load:

Instead of being charged when you make the investment, you will be charged on when you take the money out of the mutual fund. Be careful here though, because hopefully the value of your investment will be worth more when you go to redeem it than when you invested it originally. Therefore, this load could turn out to be more expensive than if you had paid a front-end load.

Deferred Load:

This works according to the time frame for which you leave the investment in the fund. The longer you leave your money in the fund, the lower the redemption charges will be when you take the investment out later.

Combination Load:

You will have a partial front-end load when you make the investment and a partial back-end load when you redeem the investment.

Negotiated Load:

This is a rare one unless you have a very large portfolio with one family of funds. It means that you negotiate the charge ahead of time outside of what is normally charged.

Specific Fee:

This one is also rare, but it means that you agree to pay a fee worth a specified percentage of your total fund value annually.

No-Load:

This means that when you invest $100.00, the whole $100.00 is being invested for you. When you redeem the investment, you aren't charged any load either.

Where Can I Find Information About My Mutual Fund?

The larger daily newspapers will carry the previous day's closing values of mutual funds in their business sections. There are also daily Canadian business newspapers which will give you the closing unit values and other business-related information that may be helpful in your investment decisions.

What Is a Simplified Prospectus and Annual Report?

These documents are very important. When you purchase a mutual fund, you should be given a copy of both the Simplified Prospectus and the Annual Report. I would suggest that before you sign anything, you ask for copies of these from your FI, investment dealer or financial advisor and read the information inside each document yourself. Some of it may seem kind of dry.

The Simplified Prospectus will give you information about management fees, sales charges (loads), details of the objectives of each fund, explanation of the risks that may be taken by the fund manager to obtain the objective, listings of who each fund manager is for each individual fund type, how to purchase units, how to withdraw or transfer units, how often income is paid on each mutual fund type, taxation information and other useful information.

The Annual Report and Semi-Annual Report provide other details of the individual funds such as the exact securities that were being held on a specific year end or semi-annual date for each fund type, various statements relating to the performance of each fund and other useful information. Even though the actual investments can change in a fund from the time the annual report is published to the time you make your investment, you can at least get an idea of the kinds of investments in which the fund will be involved.

What Is a Derivative?

Derivatives have been a hot topic in the 1990s. The rules governing derivatives in Canada are much different than those in other countries of the world. Another term for derivatives is "futures contracts." This is how it works. As an example, the fund manager is predicting that a stock market in Japan is going to be at a specific level at a future date. He purchases a million dollar contract against that prediction, or speculation. In Canada, the mutual fund must put up the whole million dollars as collateral against the contract, dollar for dollar. That way, in the future if the speculation turns out to be wrong, there are enough funds to cover the contract entirely. If the fund manager was correct, then he would receive his million dollars back plus the bonus for being correct, thus making money for the mutual fund. These contracts are bought and sold constantly every day, so the fund manager may not hold on to the contract to its maturity date. He may sell it to another investor depending on how he sees the market direction.

In other countries, contracts are often margined. This means that instead of putting up the whole million dollars as collateral, they may put up 80% of the contract value or even less. If the Japan market was very low, then when this future contract matures, the fund manager or investor will have to not only put forward the remaining 20%, but also any amount owing beyond this for being wrong in the prediction. If you get large enough amounts of money involved, low percentages of margins required and a market that goes the wrong way, this can be disastrous. This type of scenario helped bankrupt a well-established England bank in the 1990s because of one of its trader's wrong speculation.

So, derivatives worldwide can be very risky. There are a few mutual funds that use derivatives in Canada, but as stated, there is some protection according to the Canadian rules. That does not mean you can be guaranteed that a mutual fund that uses derivatives will not lose money. It can. You see, if the speculation was wrong, then a portion of that million dollars is kept by the other party which means you are losing money. This means a negative return on the mutual fund. Therefore, there is still a lot of risk involved with this type of mutual fund investment.

Are Mutual Funds Part of My Deposit Insurance With My FI?

No. A strong word of caution here: If you put $1,000.00 into a mutual fund and its value goes down to $500.00 or even $0.00 (which is theoretically possible), you are not guaranteed any of the principal amount you invested by anyone. This is a risk you must accept if you are investing in any mutual fund. Your principal is only as good as the securities or investments that the fund is holding.

Does Past Performance Indicate Future Performance?

Again, no. Just because a fund had a 30% rate of return last year does not mean it will repeat the performance. All rates of return for mutual funds are from past performance. This is historical information and should be evaluated as just that. I have seen funds go from negative rates of return to positive rates of return to negative rates of return and so on. The market conditions will dictate how a fund does, as will how the fund manager responds to these conditions. This is why dollar-cost-averaging is so important when investing in mutual funds. Unfortunately, customers see the high rates of return and state that they want the particular mutual fund that did well last year. The salesperson must indicate that past performance doesn't guarantee future performance. The salesperson should obtain enough information about you (such as age, income, net worth, tolerance to risk, etc.) that they can determine what investor style you fit and guide you towards investments which may include mutual funds that suit your investment style.

Who Do I Talk To About Purchasing Mutual Funds?

Mutual fund salespeople are licensed with the provincial government. They must take and pass an exam to be qualified to sell mutual funds. Mutual fund salespeople are highly regulated by the provincial securities commission. Almost every FI has its own team of salespeople. Financial planners, stock brokers and many life insurance companies have licensed salespeople. To do a transaction on your mutual fund, you must see a licensed salesperson. That is why when you walk into your FI or a broker's office and talk to the first person you see about mutual funds, they may ask you to wait until a licensed staff member can assist you in your request. Even if you are only requesting a copy of their mutual fund's Annual Report or Simplified Prospectus, you must talk with a licensed representative. As I said, this is highly regulated and if a non-licensed staff member gave out the mutual fund Annual Report, there would be a breach of the rules. Therefore, be patient if you are asked to wait a minute.

Are There Any Age Restrictions for Investing In Mutual Funds?

Yes, there is. You must be of the age of majority in the province of residence before you can invest in mutual funds. There is no maximum age restriction, but the older you are, the less risk you should be investing into – according to your investment style, of course.

Mutual Fund Types

$ $ $

Mutual funds range from low risk to high risk, short term to long term and Canadian content to foreign content. The following is not an all-inclusive list, but it does cover the majority of mutual fund types available in the marketplace. When considering a fund type, you should read the Simplified Prospectus carefully. A bond fund from one family of mutual funds may have a different objective than a bond fund from a different family of mutual funds. Therefore, even though the name "bond" may be the same, the investments are still two different investments and should be treated that way. At the end of this chapter, you will find the familiar risk vs. return graph as a reference.

MONEY MARKET FUND

This fund is the lowest risk vs. return mutual fund. The investments it holds are short term investments, therefore the fund is intended for short term investing. However, that does not mean you can't invest in this mutual fund for longer time frames. Examples of the types of securities the fund holds are Government of Canada T-Bills, Banker's Acceptances (short term bank notes) and high-quality short term corporate bonds. As interest rates rise and fall, the rate of return on the Money Market fund will also rise and fall.

MORTGAGE FUND

As the name states, this fund holds mortgages as investments. Many FI's have mortgage funds because they have mortgages available to choose from for the fund. For all you know, your mortgage may be in a mortgage fund and you don't even know it. Depending on the risk determined by the economy at any given point in time, this fund ranges from low to medium risk vs. return. Mortgage terms range from very short term time frames up to 5 years or more. Again, the Simplified Prospectus will tell you what parameters the fund manager must follow when selecting mortgages for this fund. Therefore, this is considered a medium time frame investment, which means 3-7 years. Economic cycles of recession to recovery can range from 3-7 years also.

You may find a few different kinds of mortgage funds. The most common is the residential first mortgage fund, which means no second mortgages are included. There are also commercial mortgage or real estate funds which are much higher risk and can be grouped with the specialty fund types.

Mortgage funds are considered a little less risky than bond funds because interest rates on the bond market can change daily whereas interest rates on mortgages usually are more stable and fluctuate less often.

Mortgage mutual funds work opposite to interest rates. To save space, refer back to the chapter entitled, "The Investor and the Investments." There was an example of "premium selling" and "discount selling." The same is true for mortgage mutual funds.

CANADIAN BOND FUND

You will find a variety of bonds in this mutual fund, including Government of Canada, provincial, corporate and mortgage-backed securities. The last one mentioned means that the specific FI has guaranteed mortgages or provided mortgages as security against the debt, often in order to obtain a better interest rate. You will also find T-Bills as part of the portfolio. You or I will use a chequing or savings account to store our excess money. A mutual fund uses T-Bills for this purpose since a mutual fund has higher amounts of money available and the ability to sell or trade on the markets easily.

A bond fund is considered a medium term investment which means a minimum 5 year time horizon. Again, refer to the section in this book that talks about premium and discount selling to get an idea of how interest rates affect bond unit values.

INTERNATIONAL BOND/INCOME FUND

Again, as the name states, this bond fund invests in international bonds. Some funds operate strictly in foreign bonds issued by foreign governments or corporations and, therefore, would be part of your foreign content in an RRSP. There are other funds that are RRSP eligible as an investment without worrying about foreign content. How can an international fund not be foreign content? Our Federal and Provincial governments, as well as some corporations, issue bonds on the market in foreign currencies in order to attract foreign investors. Since it is a Canadian government or company issuing the bond, it is considered 100% RRSP eligible, but it provides foreign currency income as part of your portfolio. Due to this second point, this fund is considered a higher risk than the Canadian bond fund because of the currency fluctuations against the Canadian dollar.

International bond funds are considered a medium term investment. Its risk is the same as the Canadian bond fund with the added risk of currency fluctuations.

DIVIDEND MUTUAL FUND

This can also be either a Canadian fund or a foreign-based fund. It invests in high quality stocks that have a track record of giving consistent dividends. You will find a lot of blue chip companies in this fund. Blue chip means well-established companies. There will be both preferred and common shares, unless the Simplified Prospectus states otherwise. As an investor, you will reap the benefits of the dividends as well as capital appreciation, which means that if the stocks go up in value, so will the unit values. Of course, the opposite is also very true. Currently, dividends are treated better than interest income when considering taxation. That is the real draw to this type of fund for an investor.

If you are considering a Canadian Dividend fund, then you can hold it inside your RRSP portfolio without concern of foreign content. Most mutual fund companies recommend that this fund type not be part of your RRSP portfolio because its objective is to provide the investor with a taxation benefit and an RRSP already has a taxation benefit on its own. However, due to its high quality investments, you can consider it for your RRSP, especially if you want to have some diversification into the stock market but only high quality investments and lower risk.

BALANCED FUND

This appears to be an unusual name for a mutual fund. However, just as you try to eat a balanced diet, the balanced fund tries to provide the investor with a selection of investments instead of only concentrating on one investment type, such as bonds. Most balanced funds contain money market securities, bonds and stocks. It will usually have foreign content of the same types of securities up to the 20% limit to maintain RRSP eligibility. The balanced fund diversifies your money for you. You can consider substituting equal amounts of bond and stock funds for balanced fund if you wish; however, this fund on its own gives you great diversification. The biggest advantage to this fund is that if the fund manager notices bonds are doing better than stocks or equities, then there is the flexibility to shift towards bonds within this fund to take advantage of this opportunity. If you are in a straight bond fund or stock fund, the fund manager doesn't have the same flexibility to respond to the markets.

Since there are stocks in the balanced fund it is considered a higher risk than bond funds, but lower risk than equity funds due to the bond content. It is considered a longer term investment of over 7 years. The money market securities will yield up and down as interest rates go up and down; bonds will follow the premium and discount selling rules and the stock or equity portion will go up and down according to the selling price of the stock on the markets at any given time.

STOCK, EQUITY AND GROWTH FUND

This type of fund can be strictly Canadian, Canadian with up to 20% foreign content, U.S. stocks only, or exclusively international stocks. Refer to the risk vs. return graph at the end of this chapter. Again, refer to the Simplified Prospectus and Annual Report for specifics about what investments the fund can invest in order to reach its objective. The main investment type you will find here are stocks. In Canada, many mutual fund companies will have at least two different Canadian stock funds. One is primarily interested in large corporations found on the Toronto Stock Exchange and foreign exchanges. The other is usually referred to as either a Growth Fund or Special Equity Fund. The stocks held here are junior companies which are in their growth stage. These are higher risk since they are not well-established companies.

In the foreign equity funds, you can find a variety of geographic mutual fund types such as US Equity, North American Equity, Asian/Pacific Equity, European Equity, to name a few. There is also the Emerging Markets or Developing Country Funds which are very high risk as you are investing in countries which are classified as the "up-and-comers, but not sure if they are going to make it." There can be sharp degrees of change in the unit values of this fund due to the market volatility associated with these emerging markets.

Any equity fund is a long term investment of over 10 years as there will be plenty of ups and downs. Therefore, dollar-cost-averaging is a must in order for you to catch the ups and downs and average out your cost to create a better rate of return for yourself.

SPECIALTY FUNDS

These funds specialize in one part of the market only and are, therefore, very risky. There is potential for very large gains, but you also have to consider very large declines. To name a few, here are some specialty funds available: Resources, Precious Metals, Technology and Derivatives. Be absolutely sure you know what you are investing in when you purchase these fund types.

OTHER FUNDS

There may be other fund types not mentioned here. My advice to you is not to get caught up in any hype about a particular mutual fund. Do your research and ask lots of questions until you understand fully what you are investing in. Track records of a mutual fund are useful, but remember that past performance is not indicative of future returns.

RISK VS. RETURN GRAPH

Why Contribute to an RRSP?

$ $ $

There are a couple of reasons to contribute to an RRSP. However, before we get to that, the initials "RRSP" stand for Registered Retirement Savings Plan. You will also see them advertised or talked about as RSP's, which stands for Retirement Savings Plan. They are one and the same because all RSP's must be registered with the Federal Government, so the "Registered" part is a given, and most FI's and writers refer to RRSP's as RSP's.

REASON #1: Because You Can Save Money Now On Your Income Taxes

None of us likes to pay more income taxes than we need to. It is true that Jesus said to pay Caesar what is due to Caesar (Matt. 22:15-22) in taxes. However, we are also to be good stewards of all that God has given us. By contributing to an RSP, you create a tax deduction which means at tax time you save yourself income tax money owed or you increase the amount of income tax payable to you as a refund. A rough calculation to see how much you would save is to take the amount you are contributing and multiply it by the tax bracket you are in. If you were in the 27% tax bracket and were contributing $1,000.00, then your tax savings would be $270.00. The higher your tax bracket the more you pay in income taxes, but also the more you can save on taxes by contributing to an RSP. If your tax bracket was 40% and you were contributing $1,000.00, then you would save $400.00 in taxes. If the income tax savings increase the amount the government owes you, then you have choices to make with this extra money. Possibly pay down some debt, contribute it back into another RSP deposit, pay down your mortgage, save for vacation, etc. Maybe consider taking some of your savings and helping others in your church or community who are not as fortunate, thus thinking more about treasures in heaven (Matt. 6:19-24) than treasures on earth. Pray about it and seek God's direction.

REASON #2: Because Your Investments Grow Tax Free

By contributing to an RSP, you are saving your money in a tax-sheltered investment until you withdraw it from your RSP plan. When the money is in an RSP, it earns income, tax free. If you tried to save money outside of your RSP, then the income generated would be taxed according to your income tax rate. If these same monies were in an RSP, the income generated would not be taxed, but would grow in the plan tax free. Only when you start to take the money out of the RSP are you then taxed on this money. There are times when saving outside of an RSP makes sense. If you are saving for a down payment on a house or for a child's education, etc., then yes, indeed, save outside of an RSP. However, if you are saving for retirement needs, then definitely save within an RSP for maximum growth potential.

REASON #3: Because It's Your Retirement You're Saving For

No doubt you have heard talk that there will not be enough CPP (Canada Pension Plan) funds available to pay out to future generations. Even if there will be enough to pay CPP and OAS (Old Age Security) to future generations, those payments don't even provide enough income for a retired person today to live comfortably. Therefore, by contributing to an RSP, you are saving for your future retirement. If CPP and OAS are still around then, these funds can be used to supplement your retirement income and lifestyle; but don't be counting on any government sponsored program to provide you with a "safety net" when you retire.

REASON #4: Because Even If You Have to Borrow the Money, It Makes Sense

Later in this book you will hear me talking about how credit or borrowing money can hurt a family because you get in over your head and can't see where to turn next. You may be at the stage where borrowing any money for anything may not make a lot of sense. However, for most people, borrowing money as an RSP loan does make economic sense. This is the one loan an FI will grant to you at prime interest rate (the best interest rate given) as long as you are depositing the funds into that FI's RSP products. If you are taking the money to invest in a competitor's RSP product, they will still entertain the loan, but at regular interest rates which could be 3% or more higher.

The following is the logic behind why it makes sense to borrow funds for an RSP contribution. Let's say your income tax rate is 40%. You are borrowing $1,000.00 at prime rate of 6% and were going to pay the loan back within 12 months with equal installments of $86.07. That $1,000.00 contribution represents a $400.00 savings on your income tax. The cost of the borrowed funds over the 12 months works out to $32.80. Therefore, your net benefit is the difference or $367.20. Plus, that $1,000.00 is earning income free of taxation over the 12 months.

Most RSP loans have to be repaid in 12 months. Some FI's do offer a 24-month repayment schedule, but at a higher interest rate. You may be asked if you want a 90-day no pay RSP loan. At first, you think great, no payments or interest for 90 days. Unfortunately, that isn't what it means. It means that you defer your first loan payment until 90 days after it was advanced. The interest still accrues (or builds up) for the 90 days. Often customers will come in on the 90th day and ask to pay off their 90-day no pay loan and be very disappointed when they see they still owe interest. It isn't a 90-day interest free no pay loan.

Why wait 90 days to pay off the loan? Most people will have their income tax return refund back within the 90 days and pay it on to the RSP loan before the 90 days is complete. This helps their cashflow for those 90 days so they don't have to worry about an extra loan payment. If you aren't planning on paying off or paying down the loan in the 90 days, that is fine too as it helps your cashflow for 90 days, but then your repayment will start with higher loan payments than if you had started paying the loan the very next month after it was advanced to you. You will have 9 months in which to pay off the total owing in this case. Plus, your interest cost will be a little more than the 12-month repayment because no reduction in principal happened for that first 3 months. Therefore, do what is best for you.

There is a large amount of unused allowable RSP contributions. This means that a lot of people have not been contributing the maximum allowed to their RSP's each year. As discussed in the next chapter, these unused balances get "carry forwards" into future years. To attract RSP investors, some FI's are now introducting longer loan terms for larger RSP loans. By doing this, you get a large tax deduction and a lower RSP loan payment.

If you borrow funds for investment purposes, the interest paid on the borrowed funds is tax deductible. However, if you borrow funds for an RSP purchase, this is one area that, even though it could be argued you are borrowing for an investment, you cannot deduct this interest paid as a tax deduction. It is viewed that the RSP itself is a 100% tax deduction, so why allow even more of a tax write-off?

REASON #5: Because Contributions Can Be Made Very Painless

With your FI or through your mutual fund company set up a plan where they will take a specific amount of money out of your account on specific dates (monthly, weekly, bi-weekly, etc.) and contribute it to your RSP plan as per your instructions. In the Mutual Fund chapters, we referred to this as dollar-cost-averaging. If you don't want mutual funds in your investment strategy, then consider having these periodic withdrawals from your chequing or savings account put into the savings section of your RSP plan. Check what the minimum term deposit amount is that your FI offers within an RSP. Most are $500.00. When you have saved the $500.00 minimum in the savings section of your RSP, then roll this over into a term deposit for a specific time frame (1 year, etc.). You are doing this because the funds in the savings section are not going to earn you as much interest income as they would if they were in a term deposit within your RSP.

What you are trying to accomplish is an easy method to save for your RSP. Set this up close to your pay days so that you don't really even miss the $50.00 or whatever you choose to contribute. Start with a small amount and gradually build the number higher as you become more comfortable with it. Eventually, you won't even need that RSP loan to top off your RSP contribution because you will be forcing yourself to save the money over the course of the year instead of having to borrow these same funds.

REASON #6: Because the Earlier You Start, the Better Off You Will Be

This is where educating ourselves so that we can educate our children comes in. This could also be called the power of compounding interest if your investments are in interest-bearing security types. The longer you wait to start contributing to an RSP, the less time you have for the investments to build tax free. It's simple. If you are 45 years old, then you have less years to retirement than a 20-year-old. Let's say retirement age is 65. On the younger person's 20th birthday, he or she contributes $1,000.00 to his or her RSP and makes no other contributions up to retirement age of 65. That initial investment at an 8% compounding annual rate of interest for 45 years will turn into $31,920.00 within a tax sheltered RSP.

The older person has only 20 years until retirement. His initial investment of $1,000.00 was put into an RSP on his 45th birthday and he made no more contributions up to age 65. That $1,000.00 at an 8% compounding annual rate of interest for 20 years will turn into $4,660.00. Very big difference. The longer it is in the plan, the better the final outcome.

Before you rush out to contribute to your RSP, whether it be an existing plan or a new plan, there are other items of interest you should know. That is what the next chapters are all about.

Things You Should Know About RSP's

$ $ $

Anything to do with Revenue Canada is often difficult to understand unless you work with their rules and policies and keep up to date on changes. Therefore, the following is general information to help you, though you may want to discuss it further directly with Revenue Canada at one of their offices or over the phone.

Definition of "Earned Income"

To contribute to an RSP you must have earned income as per the definition Revenue Canada states. This definition can change at any time. Some of the earned incomes include wages, salary and net business income. Various items that are not earned income include interest income, dividend income, capital gains, UIC premiums, CPP received and certain pension income. If there are questions about this definition, I would suggest you contact Revenue Canada.

Contribution Limit

Currently, you can contribute up to 18% of previous years earned income less any pension adjustment up to a maximum amount (which can change every year). If you belong to a pension at work or if you contribute to a pension at work, you may have a pension adjustment taken off the 18%. Unless you are an accountant or have a computer program that calculates this PA (pension adjustment), I doubt that you will want to figure it out yourself. Leave that to your employer.

The easiest method to see what you can contribute to your RSP is to find last year's income tax assessment that was mailed to you. At the bottom there is a section that tells you exactly what you can contribute after any PA. Now remember, this year's contribution is based on last year's income. So, if last year you didn't have a lot of income but this year you have a high income, you can only contribute what it states as the maximum in last year's income tax assessment. The fact that you made a lot more this year will increase how much you can contribute next year. I realize that doesn't help you a lot now when you have the higher income and want to save taxes, however, that is the rule.

Another way to find how much you can contribute is through a Revenue Canada 1-800 phone number found in the blue pages of your phone book called TIPS line.

Carry Forwards

Now, the number which represents the allowable amount you can contribute as found on the tax assessment will include not only last year's allowable, but also the previous year's allowable since you are able to carry forward any unused contributions to other years. This means that if there was a year you couldn't contribute for whatever reason or you didn't contribute the full amount you were allowed, you haven't lost the benefit. It also means that for those of you who now want to contribute to an RSP and haven't done so before, you may have a sizable carry forward built up over the years. When you do use any or all of this carry forward as a contribution, you don't re-file previous years' income taxes with the correction, but instead, it is used to reduce taxes payable in the actual year you use the carry forward. So, in the example earlier of the person who had little income in the previous year but had lots of income in the current year, if they have any carry forward, now is the time to use it up to save on income taxes for the current year.

Life-time Overcontribution

This policy has changed since it was first introduced. It used to be that you were not allowed to overcontribute to your RSP at all. If you did, and even if it was an honest mistake, Revenue Canada would make you withdraw the funds immediately or face financial penalties. Since then it has been decided to allow you room in case you do overcontribute by mistake. However, the overcontribution will not be allowed as a deduction currently, but can be used in future year(s) as a deduction. The maximum allowable is currently $2,000.00. It used to be much higher than this, but was brought down to $2,000.00 as a reasonable allowable overcontribution limit.

There are some investors who purposely overcontribute into this $2,000.00. Why? They don't receive any tax deduction currently, but the funds are earning income, tax free. However, if they wanted to take any of this overcontribution out of the RSP, they would be taxed on it, even though they never received any tax deduction benefit in the first place. Therefore, know what and why you are overcontributing if it is a planned overcontribution.

Withdrawing From Your RSP

If, for whatever reason, you need to cash in part or all of your RSP plan, be aware of a few items. First, if your RSP money is locked into a term deposit that doesn't mature for a year, as an example, the FI may not let you redeem it early. Most FI's will only do so if it can be proven that there is an emergency and you have no other choice but to cash in the RSP proceeds. If the FI proceeds, they will charge you a fee or penalty for early withdrawal of these funds due to your breaking the term contract. All withdrawals are considered taxable income. This means that at year end, you will receive a T4-RSP slip from the FI detailing the RSP withdrawal. You must include this as income on the correct line of your current income tax return. This T4-RSP slip will have two numbers on it, the first being the gross amount you withdrew, and the second being how much income tax was deducted at the source of the withdrawal, which means how much the FI was required to withhold. Revenue Canada requires that all FI's, etc. withhold a certain percentage of the RSP withdrawal and remit this to them. The following are the tax rates (may be different in Quebec) with a couple of examples:

Example: RSP Withdrawal Withholding Tax

10% for withdrawals under $5,000.00
20% for withdrawals from $5,000.00 to $15,000.00
30% for withdrawals over $15,000.00

Amount	Tax Rate	Tax Withheld	Net Proceeds
$1,000.00	10%	$100.00	$900.00
$3,000.00	10%	$300.00	$2,700.00
$5,000.00	20%	$1,000.00	$4,000.00
$10,000.00	20%	$2,000.00	$8,000.00
$12,000.00	20%	$2,400.00	$9,600.00
$15,000.00	30%	$4,500.00	$10,500.00
$20,000.00	30%	$6,000.00	$14,000.00

So that there is no confusion later, if you withdrew $3,000.00, then 10% of this, or $300.00, is being withheld as tax. You net $2,700.00 minus any fees from the FI, etc. You may still owe more tax on this withdrawal. If you are in the 40% tax bracket, then when you complete your current year's income tax, you will include the $3,000.00 as income and it will be taxed according to the tax bracket in which you are currently. Therefore, when the dust settles, you may be paying more income tax than just the $300.00 on this withdrawal. A simple way to look at it, which isn't totally accurate, is $3,000.00 x 40% = $1,200.00 in taxes. Therefore, make sure it is really worth your while to withdraw the RSP funds in the first place. There are some situations where you will have no other income for the year and, therefore, it makes sense to withdraw the RSP funds as income. If this is the case, you will have received the benefit of a tax deduction when you contributed the RSP and you may not have to pay any taxes (you will receive a refund back from Revenue Canada) on the RSP when you cash it in. Now, this isn't the purpose of an RSP, but nothing in the policies state that you can't do this.

There is a systematic way of withdrawing these RSP funds through something called an RRIF (or RIF) which stands for Registered Retirement Income Fund. More about this topic a little later.

Various Questions & Answers About RSP's

$ $ $

What Can I Invest My RSP Money In?

At your FI, you have various choices such as GIC's (Guaranteed Investment Certificates), term deposits, short term deposits (Certificate of Deposit), savings section and mutual funds. You can also invest in actual stocks and bonds if you open a self-direct RSP plan, which is discussed in another chapter. There are also many mutual fund companies available in which to invest your RSP money, and again, you may need to review the earlier chapters which discuss mutual funds.

When Can I Contribute to My RSP?

You can contribute on a systematic basis or in lump sums. Revenue Canada allows you to contribute to your RSP for up to 60 days into the following year and still have it count towards the previous year's income tax. As an example, for your 1996 taxes you can make your contribution up to and including March 1, 1997. Any contributions in 1997 after March 1st must be used in the 1997 income tax year. Any contributions between January 1, 1997 and March 1, 1997 can be used for either the 1996 tax year, as stated above, or for the 1997 tax year. You will have to calculate your taxes and see which year this contribution benefits the most.

How Do I Make My RSP Contribution?

You can go directly to your FI's branch or your financial advisor's office, or you can usually phone in your RSP contribution since most FI's and mutual fund companies have toll-free phone numbers available. If you go to your FI, you will receive your tax receipt immediately. Most others will mail you your receipt immediately.

If I Have RSP Questions Who Do I Contact?

You can talk to your FI, financial advisor or accountant. You can also phone Revenue Canada directly. Look in the blue pages of your phone book for their phone numbers.

Doesn't It Make More Sense to Pay Down Debt Instead of Contributing To an RSP?

There is no clear cut answer on this one. I could say "it depends," but that isn't enough of an answer. From my research, it appears that when interest rates are higher, it makes sense to contribute to your RSP up to the maximum allowed and apply the income tax refund towards principal reduction of debt, such as your mortgage. However, this assumes that you will receive an actual refund. Since you will need to save for retirement because the government programs will not provide what you need when you retire, I would suggest a balanced approach here. If you have $3,000.00 to apply, then put equal amounts in each. Contribute $1,500.00 towards your RSP so as to save taxes and save for your retirement, and apply the other $1,500.00 towards debt reduction. If you are paying down debt other than a mortgage, then when the debt is paid off, start a systematic plan of contributions to the RSP in place of this debt payment. If you are paying down your mortgage instead of contributing to an RSP, you will save interest costs in the end, but you will lose out on the effects of this power of compounding when it comes to long term savings for your retirement. There is a trade-off here no matter how you look at it. Some people want to get the mortgage paid off faster, which is great; however, in the 15 years spent accomplishing this goal, you will have lost 15 years of RSP contributions compounding tax free. It's a tough decision and there really isn't a right or wrong answer. However, I would suggest you balance your decision.

What Is Foreign Content In an RSP?

This topic is discussed in other chapters regarding mutual funds and self-direct RSP's. Please refer to these chapters for an explanation.

Can I Withdraw Funds From My RSP As a Down Payment On a House Purchase?

According to current government legislation, a first time home-buyer can withdraw up to $20,000.00 in total from their RSP to put towards a down payment on a house purchase where the house is your principal residence. You must be a first time homebuyer. You will be signing forms to this effect. A complete definition of what constitutes a first time homebuyer is found in the Revenue Canada booklet referred to at the end of this section. For a married couple (or common-law couple, as the government sees each as the same), each spouse can withdraw $20,000.00 from each of their total RSP plans and apply towards the house purchase as long as each is a first time homebuyer. When these funds are withdrawn in this fashion, you do not pay any income tax on the withdrawal. You will receive the full amount you withdrew up to the $20,000.00 maximum for each person.

That does not mean that you won't be taxed on the withdrawal, however. You will have 15 years to pay this withdrawal back into an RSP plan. It works out to 15 equal annual installments that must be made. Revenue Canada will send you information about this each year and there is a certain way you can claim this contribution as a home-withdrawal pay back in your income tax return. This is not a tax deduction since you received that benefit when you originally deposited the RSP proceeds. So, if you took $12,000.00 out, then you will have to repay back $800.00 per year minimum. You can pay back more than the minimum or all of it immediately, but you must at least make the minimum repayment. If you don't, then this minimum amount will become part of your income for that tax year. If you repay more than you need then this will decrease the minimum need-ed in future years. In other words, if you re-paid back $1,500.00 in the first year instead of the required $800.00, then minimum in subse-quent years will become $750.00/year ($12,000.00 − $1,500.00 = $10,500.00 divided by 14 years remaining = $750.00).

If the spouse only has a spousal plan, this can be used here also without affecting the other spouse's (the contributor's) income tax (see the chapter on spousal RSP's). As for the repayment, this is not going to sound correct, but it is the case. When the spouse starts to repay the money back into the RSP, they contribute it back to their own RSP plan and not to a spousal plan as it was originally set up.

When you do repay the RSP, you do not have to go back to the FI or mutual fund company out of which you originally took the money with these repayments. You are free to choose with whom you want to put the RSP repayment money.

Revenue Canada has published a booklet that discusses this topic which is available for the asking. It is entitled, "Home Buyer's Plan – for 199_ Participants." It is form number P150(E) for English and (F) for French. Contact Revenue Canada if you require this information.

Spousal RSP's

$ $ $

Many couples will start a spousal RSP plan in order to split their income at retirement to save taxes during retirement. This is the real purpose of a spousal RSP plan, although younger couples often plan to withdraw spousal RSP funds during times when the spouse may not be working for a time frame, such as while on maternity leave or during a leave of absence. Generally, the spouse who is earning the greater income will contribute to his or her own RSP as well as a spousal RSP. The total of what you contribute between the two cannot go above the total you are allowed to contribute as set out by Revenue Canada. You do have the choice to contribute your maximum allowed towards the spousal RSP if you wish, which means no contribution towards your own RSP. This is a consideration if you have an established pension plan or you are nearing retirement and have contributed very little to a spousal RSP. This spouse may have his or her own personal RSP plan, but any spousal contributions must be put into a separate plan other than the personal plan.

Example: RSP Contribution – Spousal

Maximum allowed according to Revenue Canada: $4,600.00
Choice #1:   Contribute maximum allowed to your RSP = up to $4,600.00
Choice #2:   Contribute maximum allowed to spousal RSP = up to $4,600.00
Choice #3:   Contribute maximum allowed between your personal RSP and the spousal RSP = up to $4,600.00

There is a big misunderstanding when it comes to withdrawing funds from a spousal RSP. Revenue Canada has set out a 3-year rule for withdrawals. Remember that the reason you are contributing to a spousal RSP is to income split for the future so as to reduce income taxes. The spousal contribution must remain in a spousal plan for 3 calendar years from the last time a contribution was made at any FI or any spousal RSP plan anywhere in Canada. What does that statement mean? The following chart is an example showing all the spousal contributions made.

Example: 3-Year Spousal Withdrawal Rule

Date	Contribution	Withdrawal	Plan Value	Where Contributed
Jan. 1994	$3,500.00		$3,500.00	Wonderful Bank
Feb. 1995	$2,000.00		$5,500.00	Bank of that Town
Dec. 1996	$1,000.00		$6,500.00	Credit Union Anytown
Jan. 1999		$6,500.00	$0.00	
Feb. 2000	$4,000.00		$4,000.00	This Trust Co.
Feb. 2001	$1,500.00		$5,500.00	ABC Mutual Fund
Jul. 2002		$3,000.00	$2,500.00	

The example doesn't include the income generated by the RSP investments. For a spousal RSP to work, there has to be two spouses. One is called the contributing spouse and the other the planholder spouse. For the years 1994, 1995 and 1996, the contributing spouse would deduct the contributions from his or her income tax. The planholder spouse still owns the money, however, and has free rein on how it is to be invested. In 1999, when the withdrawal was made, whose income is it according to Revenue Canada? The three-year rule states that the spousal contribution can be withdrawn and taxed in the spouse's hands after 3 tax calendar years have expired since the last contribution to any spousal RSP plan. The last contribution in the example was December 1996. So you count the three calendar years as follows: 1996 counts as the first tax year, 1997 is the second and 1998 is the third tax year. No, the money didn't sit there for 3 whole years because that isn't what the rule states. In 1999, at any time, unless a contribution is made to the spousal plan in that year, any of the funds withdrawn will be taxed in the hands of the spouse (planholder) and not the contributor.

Now, back to our example. In the years 2000 and 2001, there were further contributions made by the contributor to the spouse's RSP plan. Then in 2002, a withdrawal was made on the plan. In this case,

99

the withdrawal would be taxed in the hands of the contributor and not the spouse (planholder) because the 3-year rule hadn't expired. This income would have to be added to any other income the contributor has that year and taxed in the tax bracket of the contributor for that year. This is why you must be careful about the 3-year rule for spousal plan withdrawals.

The only time the 3-year rule is not enforced is either upon death of the planholder spouse who owns the spousal plan or when converting the RSP to an RIF. For the RIF, see a separate chapter on this as there are special requirements.

If you are doing spousal plan contributions, you should be very aware that the spouse controls the money in the plan. This means that if the planholder spouse withdrew the money at the wrong time, it could affect the contributor's taxes. Unfortunately, if there is a marriage breakdown, the planholder spouse may need funds and decide to cash in the spousal RSP plan, which they are allowed to do because they own the plan and the money in the plan. If the three years has not expired, then this money will still be taxed in the contributor's hands and not the planholder spouse's hands, even though this spouse received the actual money.

Spousal RSP's are a great idea to save taxes in the future. However, be very aware of the rules surrounding them.

Self-Direct RSP

$ $ $

A self-direct RSP means that you as the investor are similar to a fund manager of a mutual fund in that you make the investment choices as to what will form your total RSP portfolio. You have the ability to consolidate all of your RSP plans from all of the FI's and mutual fund companies you deal with into one plan as one portfolio.

You have greater control as to what you want in your RSP. You have choices from all the RSP investments discussed in the previous chapters: Canadian mutual funds, individual stocks and bonds, Canada Savings Bonds, foreign stocks, bonds and mutual funds and even a personal residential mortgage.

The foreign content rule relates to your total self-direct plan value. In other words, you can have various mutual funds from various mutual fund families in your plan, plus Canadian and foreign stocks, etc., as long as when you add up your total portfolio there is no more than 20% in foreign content. As a refresher, refer to the chapter, "Mutual Funds – Questions and Answers," that discussed RSP's and foreign content.

Example: Self-Direct RSP Portfolio

Investment Type	Value of Investment	Foreign Content
200 shares ABC Co.	$6,800.00	No
Canada Savings Bonds	$4,500.00	No
Gov't Canada 10-year Bond	$20,000.00	No
DEF Mutual Fund-Cdn. Bond	$1,500.00	No
GHI Mutual Fund-Cdn. Stock	$4,000.00	No
JKL Mutual Fund-US Equity	$4,000.00	Yes
MNO Mutual Fund-Int'l Equity	$2,000.00	Yes
100 shares PQR Co. (Japan)	$2,500.00	Yes
Total Plan Value:	$45,300.00	
Total Foreign Content:	$8,500.00	18.8% of Total Plan Value

If you have a share certificate for XYZ Company worth $1,500.00 outside of your self-direct RSP, then the income generated from this investment is paid to you directly and you are taxed each year on that income accordingly. If that share certificate was in your self-direct RSP, then the income generated from the investment is paid to your self-direct RSP. This means the income is tax-sheltered income until you decide to withdraw funds from your self-direct RSP portfolio.

The advantage of a self-direct RSP is that you make the decisions. You can buy or sell securities yourself. Also, since all your RSP's are under the same plan or portfolio, record keeping is streamlined and easier to understand. Disadvantages are that you must have enough knowledge to make your own investment decisions and you must take the time to monitor your investments.

Every FI has a self-direct plan for which you can apply to open. Be aware that there is usually an annual administration fee that is payable to the FI. Any trading activity that you do, such as purchasing or selling stocks on the markets, will cost you brokerage fees. Make sure you investigate these costs before you open a self-direct RSP plan. It is advisable that if your self-direct plan is less than $15,000.00 in portfolio balance, any fees you pay may not be justified. There could be cases when this isn't true. Some people have investments such as stocks that are held outside their RSP as an investment. If they are cash-strapped for an RSP contribution, they may consider opening a self-direct plan and depositing the share certificates into the plan as a contribution in order to obtain an income tax receipt. If this is done, then the share certificates are now RSP money. If you wanted to cash in the share certificates to obtain cash for yourself, then you would do so through your RSP self-direct plan, but you would also pay income tax on the withdrawal because those certificates are now part of your RSP plan. Therefore, be careful of what investments you place in your self-direct plan.

Many FI's have either or both a discount brokerage and a full brokerage service available to self-direct RSP investors. Discount brokerage means you will receive no advice or information about your investments. You pay a reduced cost in comparison to the full brokerage service. However, you have to do your own research and know for yourself what you are investing in. The full service brokerage provides you with research information and advice. You do pay more in your trading costs for this extra service. Therefore, weigh the pros and cons here. Are you doing enough trading to warrant a full service brokerage and have a high enough RSP balance in your self-direct plan to justify the costs? Or do you know what you want to invest in from your own knowledge and research and, therefore, only need a discount brokerage service? Make sure you are receiving enough value out of the costs incurred.

It was mentioned earlier that you could hold a personal residential mortgage in your self-direct RSP. This is not for everyone. Each FI will have its own guidelines, so further research is a must. What you are doing is placing your personal mortgage on your personal residence as an investment inside your self-direct RSP. You make mortgage payments to the self-direct RSP, or yourself really, at the specified interest rate for a stated term and amortization. A mortgage is a "debt instrument" just as a bond or stock is also a debt instrument. The interest generated from your payments goes back into your plan as income. The interest plus the principal repayment of the payments can be used to invest in other investments within the self-direct plan.

When interest rates are high, this type of investment may make sense. If you locked in for a 5-year term at a high interest rate and interest rates went down, then this was a good investment. If you are reaping the income from your own mortgage, you don't mind if rates go down because you are paying yourself, tax sheltered. When interest rates are low, this investment is less likely considered for an RSP, although the rate of return may still be higher than other investment options.

This may sound like a great idea, but there are some things to be considered. The first is whether you have enough self-direct RSP plan value to actually do this. If your total self-direct plan added up to $100,000.00 and you wanted the mortgage to be $75,000.00, then you would have to sell off at least $75,000.00 of the existing securities you are holding and then put the mortgage in its place for $75,000.00. The initials SDRSP mean self-direct RSP.

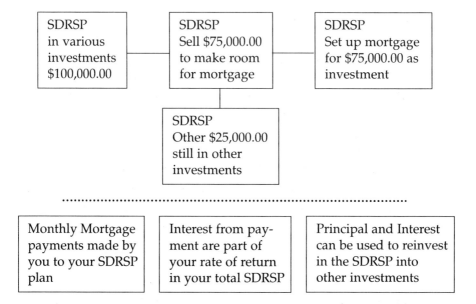

There are costs involved in doing this type of transaction. Here are some of the costs: appraisal cost, legal fees, annual mortgage fee since it is in an SDRSP, possible set-up fee and possible mortgage default insurance fee. Your total return had better be worth the costs to make this a practical choice for your RSP plan. A mortgage as part of your SDRSP is definitely not an investment choice for everyone. All the details surrounding this type of transaction are not included in this book. It is strongly suggested that you contact your FI to discuss this as an investment alternative for your SDRSP.

A self-direct RSP plan may or may not be best for you. It is a personal decision. Do your research and make sure you can justify any costs you will incur against the income generated from the plan. You want to ensure that your rate of return is still acceptable after you subtract all costs in operating the plan.

Annuities

$ $ $

Currently, by the end of the year in which you turn 71, you must convert your RSP savings into either an RIF or an annuity. As you will note in the RIF chapter, these rules are changing in 1997, so be aware. Your other choice is to simply cash in all your RSP's in one lump sum, but this could prove to be a very expensive tax liability. In the next chapter, we will discuss the RIF product.

For an annuity, you take your RSP portfolio and purchase from a life insurance company a guaranteed income for life or specific time frame and they are given all of your RSP portfolio in exchange. For the life annuity, you know for certain that regular payments of income will be coming your way. The other advantage is that you are guaranteed that your investments will not run out because the life insurance company has promised you consistent payments for your whole life. The life insurance company's plan is to take your RSP money, guarantee you a specific rate of return for the rest of your life, and then invest your money (which is now their money) in order to make an even better rate of return. The spread between what they are paying you and what they can make in the marketplace is profit to them. Also, if for whatever reason you die, even if it was only the next year, then the life insurance company keeps the remaining proceeds.

In order to guard against this, you could set up what is referred to as a joint and last survivor annuity. This means that if the person who is receiving the annuity payments dies, then their spouse will receive continued payments until their death. You will be paid a lesser payment than in the first example for this added benefit. However, upon death of the second spouse, there is no further beneficiary allowed which means the life insurance company could reap the benefits if both spouses died earlier than expected.

There are also fixed term annuities. These provide regular income but only for a specified time frame. If an early death does occur, then the beneficiary or estate will receive a specified lump sum.

For details on annuities, you are advised to talk with your life insurance agent. The advantage to an annuity is regular payments to you and to your spouse if so chosen until death. The disadvantages include lack of protection against inflation increases (ie. you may receive a better rate of return if you managed the funds instead of the insurance company) and fixed payments which are inflexible if you ever needed extra funds in an emergency. Whenever interest rates are low in the markets, it is harder to sell annuities. Who wants to lock in to an annuity that is paying only a low percent for the rest of your life? Those who locked in to an annuity back when interest rates were very high (remember the 1980s) are still doing well and made a good choice at that time, as long as they can outlive the annuity if they took a life annuity.

RIF

$ $ $

The initials for this can be either RRIF or RIF. They stand for Registered Retirement Income Fund. As stated in the Annuity chapter, currently, you must convert your RSP money into either an annuity or RIF by the end of the year you turn 71 years old. However, this rule is changing in 1997. From 1997 onwards, the age limit has been reduced to 69. What this means is that if you are 69, 70 or 71 by December 31, 1997 you must convert your RSP over to an annuity or RIF product by December 31, 1997. This is a law set out by Revenue Canada. In the future, you may see pressure to make the minimum age even lower since the baby boom generation is approaching retirement. The reason for this is that a large amount of money sits in RSP balances and has been accumulating tax free for so many years. If the government reduces the minimum age, this money will be available to be taxed all the sooner. This could help the government fund the CPP costs as these will sky rocket when the baby boomers reach retirement.

Of all the choices available for your RSP funds, the RIF product is the most common now. You should note that you don't have to be 69 or 71 to put your RSP money into an RIF.

RIF Advantages

There are many advantages to an RIF. You decide where the tax-sheltered money (your previous RSP funds) is to be invested which means you reap the benefits of your decisions. Of course, if you make any poor choices this will affect your rate of return. You will have a variety of investment choices available to you from GIC's to mutual funds. There are even some self-direct RIF's available if you want individual stocks and bonds as part of your portfolio. Your RIF funds

107

are allowed to continue to grow tax-sheltered until they are withdrawn. If you die, your beneficiary or estate will receive the remaining RIF balance. You can hedge yourself against inflation with your investment choices. You must receive a minimum payment as stated by Revenue Canada (see chart), but you have the flexibility to take more out of your RIF if necessary to cover expenses, vacation or an emergency. To sum up the benefits of an RIF, it is very flexible to meet your needs since you can custom design it.

Minimum RIF Payments

Revenue Canada has set specific rules about the minimum amount you must withdraw from your RIF on an annual basis. You can receive the RIF payments monthly or however, but over the course of a calendar year, there is a minimum that must have been paid to you from your RIF funds. It used to be that the RIF must be finished by the age of 90. Now it goes beyond that age. Your minimum is based on the balance in your RIF at the end of the previous year. For an example (refer to the schedule), if you are 75 years old (on January 1st of this year) and the year end RIF balance last year was $200,000.00, then the minimum you must take out this year is $15,700.00. You can take more than this out, but this is the minimum.

Now, a feature that you can take advantage of if you have a spouse who is younger than you is to base the minimum payment on your spouse's age instead of your own. So, in our example, you are 75 but your spouse is 70. That would mean that the minimum you must take out is $200,000.00 x 5.00% = $10,000.00. When you first set up your RIF, you will be asked whose age you are basing the minimum payment on. Once your choice has been made, you cannot change it back to the other method.

According to current Revenue Canada rules, payments of your RIF are eligible for the income tax credit of $1,000.00 if you are 65 years or older. Make sure you claim this if you are eligible in order to save yourself income tax.

Schedule of Minimum RIF Payment Percentages

Your Age at Start of the Year	Minimum Payment Percentage
55	2.86
56	2.94
57	3.03
58	3.13
59	3.23
60	3.33
61	3.45
62	3.57
63	3.70
64	3.85
65	4.00
66	4.17
67	4.35
68	4.55
69	4.76
70	5.00
71	7.38
72	7.48
73	7.59
74	7.71
75	7.85
76	7.99
77	8.15
78	8.33
79	8.53
80	8.75
81	8.99
82	9.27
83	9.58
84	9.93
85	10.33
86	10.79
87	11.33
88	11.96
89	12.71

90	13.62
91	14.73
92	16.12
93	17.92
94 plus	20.00

Most FI's can print you off an RIF payment schedule if you want to see one based on a specific dollar figure.

Spousal RIF's

In the chapter about spousal RSP's, you were referred to this chapter for further explanation. Let's say that the contributing spouse made a contribution to the planholder's RSP the year before the planholder converted this spousal RSP into an RIF. According to the rules, you would think that any funds withdrawn would be taxed back to the contributor. This is not so only if the planholder spouse receives just the minimum payment. If any extra is withdrawn before the 3-year rule expires, then this excess amount will be taxed back in the contributor's hands. So, be careful.

Summary of Investments

$ $ $

- You don't need a lot of money to be an "investor," although you do need to know what investments are available, what their features and benefits are and how they respond to the financial marketplace.

- Study the risk vs. return graph so you know where your risk tolerance is placed.

- Be aware of the risks associated with investing, such as market timing, interest rate, cashability, currency and advice risks.

- Determine which investment style or approach you are and keep focused on it when you are making investment decisions.

- Mutual Funds can be a difficult subject to understand. Refer back to the questions and answers as a refresher.

- Be certain you understand that mutual fund investing is not for everyone. No matter which mutual fund you choose to invest in, it has no guarantees, so fully understand what you are investing in before you invest.

- Part of the understanding of mutual funds is knowing their features, benefits and how they respond to the financial marketplace. Understand where the mutual fund type fits into the risk vs. return graph.

- Six reasons are provided to answer the question of "Why contribute to an RRSP?"

- There are a lot of things you need to know about RSP's before you start investing in them. You also need to know details about when you want to withdraw them.

- Other questions and answers about RSP's are presented to give some guidance.

- Spousal RSP's are a great method to income split for retirement; however, understand the rules that surround them.

- Self-Direct RSP's are useful for more sophisticated investors who want to be in control of their investments, but who are also willing to spend the time to manage them.

- There will come a time when your RSP savings will have to be converted into either an annuity or an RIF. Each product has its pros and cons. The majority of people choose the RIF due to its added flexibility.

Borrowing Money – Personal Lending

$ $ $

Topics relating to borrowing money by way of a credit card, personal loan or line of credit will be addressed in this section. There will be specific advice provided ranging from what is needed for the meeting with the loans officer to what risks to be aware of when borrowing money.

Do not love the world or anything in the world. If anyone loves the world, the love of the Father is not in him. For everything in the world – the cravings of sinful man, the lust of his eyes and the boasting of what he has and does – comes not from the Father but from the world. The world and its desires pass away, but the man who does the will of God lives forever.

1 John 2:15-17

Borrowing Money

$ $ $

There are many forms of credit, or borrowing money, which will be discussed in this next section. Most of us use one form of credit or another in our daily lives, whether it be on our credit card, for a loan, line of credit or mortgage. Unfortunately, many people have let credit control their lives and are now faced with many uncertainties about how they are going to pay every creditor back.

There are a growing number of individuals and families that have such immense stress financially that they remind me of the can of pop I once left on the back seat of my car. I forgot all about it while the hot summer sun beat through the window of the parked vehicle until the can couldn't hold the pressure anymore, and yes, exploded cola everywhere inside of my car! Uncontrolled debt can lead very easily into family problems which, if not dealt with, could lead to a family crisis. Difficulties between parents and children, and especially strained relationships between husband and wife result. All too often in my line of work we are informed of another couple divorcing, which is upsetting and very unsettling. Finances may not be the only reason for the marriage breakdown, but more often than not it plays a large role.

Let me urge you, if you are just starting out on your own or have just been married, to vow to yourself, and if married, to your mate, that you will live within your means. That doesn't mean you will never borrow money, because in our society today credit plays an important role. However, it does mean that you will be responsible and good stewards of all that God has given to you.

The paradox of credit is that the approval for credit is based solely on information about you up to that day you applied. But 5 years, 1 month or even a day later, your circumstances can change to such a degree that if you applied for that same credit you would be denied. However, even if circumstances change, you still have that credit available to you, which only if abused will be taken away from you. You see, the FI granting the personal credit rarely checks up on you every year or month, and definitely not daily. As long as they are being paid, there is no need to contact you.

Credit is granted and you are to be responsible with it. You are also to be responsible to know how much credit is enough. Don't rely solely on the FI or credit card company to tell you this. They rely on you paying your bills with the interest so that they make money from you. In order to satisfy the human desire for "more of something now," credit grantors will put you to the limits if allowed. Very rarely is any counseling on debt provided from the credit grantor. They simply expect you to know what you are doing. Do you feel this confident?

So then, how much credit is too much? You will see when we talk about mortgages that it is recommended that a maximum of 40-42% of your combined "gross income" should be used to pay all debts including the mortgage payment and property taxes. Gross income is the income paid to you before any taxes, etc. are taken off. However, with taxation rates as high as they are and with all the other taxes we pay in life, including GST, plus the cost of food, utilities, etc., then this percentage stated may be too high.

Example:

Consider a person with gross earnings of $40,000.00. After allowance for tax credits (deductions), this person pays about 30% in combined federal and provincial taxes and the cost for UIC and CPP. So, before seeing any of the income, approximately 30% of it is gone. That leaves 70% to pay everything else (which includes the other taxes of GST, etc.). So, if the debt load added up to 40%, then this person has only 30% (70 - 40 = 30) of the original gross income left to live off. This means $12,000.00 per year or 1,000.00 per month. That $1,000.00 is to pay for the utilities, clothing, fuel, food, etc. Therefore, any money saved from going into debt certainly helps the cash flow picture.

As you can see, budgeting is very important here. If you have prepared and use a budget (refer to Section 1 of this book), then you know where your money is going. You will be able to see quickly how any further debt will affect your day-to-day living. The problem is that most people don't know where their money is going in the first place, so they don't know when to say "no more" or "stop, enough is enough" when it comes to credit.

Respect debt. Get a handle on your debt load before it takes control of you and becomes instrumental in causing hardship to you and others. We all need discipline when it comes to both saving money and spending money. Re-read the verses that started this section in 1 John. Most buying decisions are brought on by what we see – use of our senses. It can cloud what we really know to be true. Before you know it, your desire is fulfilled. But at what expense? As stated earlier in Section 1 of this book, step back and take your time when making purchase decisions. As a Christian, always remember that we are on this earth to do God's will, not to satisfy all of our worldly cravings.

This verse also speaks about boasting. One trap we fall into is looking at our neighbours and judging ourselves against their worldly possessions. The size of a house, the number and types of vehicles in a driveway, or a job title does not necessarily mean someone has it made and is successful. Most times, what a person appears to own is a façade. They may appear to "own" lots of nice things, but are really financing all of it beyond their personal means just to appear as if they are successful in this world. I have counseled and seen many of these "successful" people lose everything financially and personally because they couldn't control their spending and debt habits.

Habits often start when we are young. It comes from our own experiences as well as the example of those we grow up with. We need to teach our children self-control about wants and be a living example to them of good stewardship with all that God has given to us. Remember that self-control is one of the fruits of the Spirit stated in Galatians 5:22-26. Like anything in life, debt is not necessarily a bad thing. It is uncontrolled debt which doesn't fit into your plan of needs in life that will cause the most anguish, heartache and stress. Be careful.

This section will give guidance to what the features and benefits (and drawbacks) of the various forms of credit are, as well as details about each product type so you can be well informed when you walk into your FI or elsewhere to apply for credit.

Credit Interview

$ $ $

Often when you enter your FI for an appointment with a lending officer, you aren't sure of what to expect. As a banker, I have shaken many sweaty palms when I approach the waiting area and introduce myself. This experience can be very nerve-wracking, especially if it is your first time. It's almost like a job interview. What are they going to ask me? What if I say something wrong? What if I can't answer a question?

The discussion will start with you explaining why you called for the interview in the first place. Then the FI's representative will start asking lots of questions. In order to have yourself prepared ahead of the interview, complete the worksheet at the end of this chapter before you enter the appointment. By completing this, it will make you more confident about who you are, what you own and what you perhaps owe. It will also show the lending officer that you have taken the time to organize yourself.

There may be discussion about your credit bureau. There are credit agencies that keep track of when you seek credit, where you were seeking it and on what date. These same agencies are reported to by almost every creditor in Canada about what credit facilities you have with them, when you opened that credit, what was the beginning balance, what your balance is now, have you ever been late and if so when and how many times, plus how severe, or how late, were you (30 days, 60 days, 90 days or was the debt written off completely)? Other information such as collections against you, judgments, credit related court actions and bankruptcies are all recorded in a person's credit bureau file. You can see your own file or usually discuss it over the phone with the credit bureau agency if you want to check up on your credit or if you have any questions regarding what your FI tells you about your credit bureau. You may have to ask your FI which credit bureau agent they use if you want to pursue this. If you are new to credit, you may not have a credit bureau report yet.

What you have done in the past with your credit will affect you into the future. Items remain on your credit bureau until 7 years from after they have been settled. In other words, if you had a collection 5 years ago and you paid it 1 year ago, that collection will still show as a derogatory item on your credit bureau for another 6 years. You could say it will be held against you even though restitution has taken place. Be very careful how you handle your credit because your complete credit history is being recorded for review and scrutinizing by your FI. Derogatory information will lessen your chances of being approved for your credit request.

The interview is also a time for you to ask questions. If you don't understand something, then ask. Don't leave with any misunderstandings. Phone the lending officer back if a question comes up after the interview is ended and you have had time to think.

With the age of computers comes a more streamlined approach to lending. The information you provide your FI is entered into their computer. More and more now this information is scored by the computer and an answer of "approved" or "not approved" comes back while you are sitting in the FI's office. Less and less does the person you are talking to have a say in whether your personal credit application is approved or not. If you don't get enough "points," then you won't be approved. Your job tenure, type of employment, credit bureau rating, length of time at current residence, etc. are all given points. If you don't reach the minimum, then the computer will decline you. Not all FI's are this way, but they are heading in this direction. When credit scoring is mastered by the FI, then you can enter your own application on computer and see your score of approved or not approved without talking to a person. Sound unrealistic? I have learned one definite thing in my career as a banker – anything is possible. What you thought was impossible only two years ago is reality today.

Many times the lending officer will need time to evaluate your application and will contact you with the decision. With the system mentioned above, you will know right away what the decision is.

When making your appointment with the FI, ask what income verification they will need. Some will want your most recent pay stub, others your latest T-4 slip or letter of employment from your employer. If you are self-employed, you will probably need either the last 2-3 years of personal income tax returns or notices of assessments and/or financial statements of your company for the last 2-3 years.

The interview process can appear to be a scary event, but the more you are prepared for it, the easier it should be. Complete the following CREDIT APPLICATION WORKSHEET to prepare yourself.

CREDIT APPLICATION WORKSHEET

PERSONAL INFORMATION:

_____ _____ _____ _____ _____
Last Name   First Name   Initial   Social Insurance Number   Birth Date (Y/M/D)

Mailing/Physical Address:

_____
Box/Apt./Suite/R.R. #   Street # and Name   City   Prov.   Postal Code

How long have you lived at this address? _____ years.

If less than 3 years, please state previous addresses:

_____ = _____ years.

_____ = _____ years.

Home Phone #: (____) ____ - _____ Work Phone #: (____) ____ - _____

_____ _____ _____ _____ _____
Spouse's Last Name   First   Initial   Social Insurance Number   Birth Date (Y/M/D)

EMPLOYMENT INFORMATION:

_____
Employer's Name   Your Occupation   Phone Number   Years Employed

What is your gross monthly income? $_____

Are you F/T, P/T, Casual or Seasonal? _____

Are you self-employed? _____ (Y/N) If so, for how long? _____ years.

If less than 5 years at present employer, please list previous employers:

_____

_____

_____
Employer's Name   Your Occupation   Phone Number   Years Employed

Spouse's Employment:

_____
Employer's Name   Your Occupation   Phone Number   Years Employed

What is your gross monthly income? $_____

Are you F/T, P/T, Casual or Seasonal? _____

Are you self-employed? _____ (Y/N) If so, for how long? _____ years.

Other Sources of Income:

_____ _____
Source of Income (Pension/RIF/Rental income, etc.)   Monthly Income Amount

YOUR PERSONAL ASSETS, LIABILITIES AND NET WORTH

List all personal bank accounts:

_____

_____

_____

Financial Institution	Bank Account #	Balance $	Chequing/Savings

Assets:			
Total Cash in Bank Accounts:		$	_Any other details about_
Listing of Stocks/Bonds/Mutual Funds:			_Assets can be written here if_
*		$	_not enough room available:_
*		$	
Term Deposits/Savings Bonds			
*		$	
*		$	
RSP's (where and maturity date):			
*		$	
*		$	
Other Investments (provide details):			
*		$	
Automobiles-Personal (Yr/Make/Model):			
*		$	
*		$	
Other Assets-Collectibles, Furnishings:			
*		$	

Real Estate				
Principal Residence Present Value:	$		**Mortgage**	
How much is owing on mortgage?	$		Monthly Payment Amt:	$
Where is mortgage? _____			Monthly Property Taxes:	$
If have 2nd mortgage, how much?	$		Strata Fee (condo):	$
Where is 2nd mortgage? _____			What is your interest rate?	%
Value of house after mortgages:		$	When is maturity date?	
Rental Property Present Value:	$		Monthly Payment Amt:	$
How much is owing on mortgage?	$		Monthly Property Taxes:	$
Where is mortgage? _____			Strata Fee (condo):	$
Value of house after mortgage:		$	When is maturity date?	
Other Real Estate Owned (details):				
*		$		
TOTAL ASSETS		$		

Liabilities:	Balance	Monthly Payment	Any collateral held against this debt?
List your Credit Cards:			
*	$	$	
*	$	$	
*	$	$	
List any Personal Loans:			
*	$	$	
*	$	$	
*	$	$	
List any Personal Line of Credit:			
*	$	$	
*	$	$	
Other Debts You Have:			
*	$	$	
*	$	$	
From Assets Section:			
Bal. owing Principal Residence	$	$	Full Monthly Paym't
Bal. owing Principal Residence 2nd	$	$	Full Monthly Paym't
Bal. owing Rental Property	$	$	Full Monthly Paym't
Rent/Room & Board/Other		$	
Total Liabilities & Total Paym'ts	**$**	**$**	

Net Worth:	
Total Assets	$
Minus Total Liabilities	$
Equals Net Worth	$

What credit product are you applying for? _____

How much money do you need? _____

How soon do you need this financing? _____

Is this application in your name only or jointly with spouse? _____

If you were to need a co-signor (who is equally as responsible for your loan as you are), who would that person be? _____

Any other information you feel is useful towards this credit application?

_____

Risks of Credit Card Debt

$ $ $

Of all the forms of debt available, credit card debt is the easiest to obtain, the hardest to control and the most difficult to pay back. Every FI, department store, hardware store, electronics store, furniture store, gas station, etc. wants you to have their credit card in your wallet or purse available to use instantly when you see that item you just can't do without and must have now. There are many risks associated with credit cards which each person has to consider before they sign the credit card application.

Convenience Borrowing Risk

Throughout this book, I refer to the eyes as being the great deceiver. Just refer to the events in the Garden of Eden. When it comes to convenience borrowing, you had better have very good self-control and discipline because the temptation to spend can be instantly fulfilled by pulling out that piece of plastic called a credit card and presenting it to the clerk as a "form" of payment for goods or services. If you really want something bad enough, the convenience is available. The credit card issuer would like you to borrow on impulse because then, if you can't pay it back all at once by the due date on the bill, you owe them interest on what you borrowed.

Family Relations Risk

Both sexes are vulnerable to spending money with convenience borrowing. In my office, I hear the wife talk about how her husband spends without thinking with their credit cards. There is also the husband who is frustrated because he wants his wife to be happy, but her spending habits with the credit cards troubles him. Communication and leadership are necessary here. I didn't say verbal judgment or dictatorial authority. You may need help from an outside source who can help counsel you together through this process. Action should be taken, otherwise spending on convenience borrowing will snowball into possible financial hardship, plus all the other spin-off effects such as family breakdown.

The World's Myth Risk

The world would have you think that you can't live without convenience borrowing. These days you can't rent a car or a video or book airplane tickets without a major credit card. The world wants you to feel jealous that someone else has that gold credit card, so you had better have one too so that you appear as successful as they do. This is why you must portray self-control and discipline. If you really need a credit card, then fine, use it, but don't abuse it. I know of many people who store their major credit cards in their safe deposit boxes or in the freezer so that they don't have easy access to them. They will use their card only if necessary, as in the instance of booking a flight. There are others who simply go through life without using a credit card at all, either because they don't need one or because they have witnessed the devastating effects of convenience borrowing in the past and don't want to go through that again. However, these are a rarity.

Interest Rate Risk

For the convenience of walking around with open-ended credit, up to the limit on the credit card, of course, the card issuer will normally charge you a higher rate of interest than for a loan or a line of credit. The retail store type credit cards will have the highest interest rate costs. Avoid carrying any debt on these cards due to their higher expense to you. Study your credit card bills sometime and see how much interest you pay on any unpaid balance. The major credit card companies usually have a variety of cards to select from with different interest rates on each card style. Some cards will offer you lower interest rates, but you pay an annual fee for the card. If you carry a balance, then this fee can sometimes be worthwhile to pay in order to obtain the preferred interest rate. This is where you need to research.

Since credit card debt carries the highest interest rate of all the kinds of debt, you should concentrate on paying it down as quickly as possible. That doesn't mean you shouldn't be paying your other debts in a timely manner just so that the credit card debt is paid off sooner. It means that any extra funds you have should be put towards credit card debt reduction before paying down a loan or mortgage debt because of its higher interest rate.

Repayment Risk

Most credit cards require a minimum payment. This can range from 3-5% with the odd card requiring you to pay off the whole balance every month. The first risk here is whether you are able to make the minimum payment required on all your credit cards. If you are carrying a balance on each of your credit cards, then your payment on this debt should be part of your budget you prepared. Otherwise, you run the risk of getting behind on your payments which could harm your credit rating.

The second repayment risk is whether you will be able to pay the credit card debt off in total or will it always be a lingering problem and feel like the never-never plan of making only minimum payments for years. Consider talking to your FI about a consolidation loan of all your credit card debts. If approved, you should pay off all the credit card debt into the loan and close the credit cards. You can consider keeping one major credit card, but at a reduced limit of say $1,000.00. The consolidation loan will be at a cheaper rate of interest and you can put the loan over a time frame that you know will eventually pay it off in full. If the FI can't approve you for a consolidation loan, then consider paying off your most expensive credit cards into your least expensive credit card – of course, I am assuming you have available credit on your least expensive credit card – and return the higher rate credit card(s) back to their issuer requesting the account to be closed. By doing this, you will save yourself some interest expense as well as make administering your credit card debt easier because you will have less credit card companies to pay each month.

Too Many Credit Cards Risk

In the mail, we all receive information and applications to apply for credit. When we walk into department stores or our FI, we are faced with credit opportunities. What gets a lot of people into cash-flow trouble is having too many credit cards which results in too much temptation which then results in too many balances to pay back. You should be able to get through life with one or two major credit cards. The major credit cards are suggested here because they usually have lower interest rates and are accepted almost everywhere. Of course, the less number of credit cards and the lower your credit limits you have, the further ahead you will be. Most major credit cards come with specific features and benefits to lure you to use their card. This will be discussed in the next chapter. If this attracts you, then choose the one or two credit cards that give you the benefits you desire.

Credit Rating Risk

If you don't pay back your credit card debt in an orderly and timely fashion, you will be hurting your chances of obtaining credit in the future. You see, good and bad repayment of debt is recorded on your personal credit bureau. If you have had no problems in the past paying back your debts in a timely fashion – in other words, before or on the due date – this will show as a positive item on your credit bureau. If you are over 30 days late or more for your payments, this will also be recorded on your credit bureau. You run the risk of both embarrassment and future inability to obtain credit when you may really need it, such as for your first mortgage. As discussed in the previous chapter, how you handle your credit will remain on your credit bureau for 7 years, which when you really think about it, is a long time frame since a lot can happen in a 7-year period in a person's life.

Final Comments

Think of your credit card(s) as a fishing pole. On the hook or lure is the bait of temptation to spend for "wants," as well as spend on your credit card to earn more "benefits" in the form of points towards airfare, merchandise, etc. The merchant will try to "bait" you with his merchandise. You control how much bait you will accept. Attached to the lure is a fishing line. The more you spend with the credit card(s), the further the line goes out – until you run out of line, of course, which means you are potentially in deep trouble. The fishing pole starts out being in your control. But then, if you spend on your credit cards uncontrollably, the ownership of the fishing pole goes to the credit card company, since you owe the money now. You need to take the fishing pole and control the amount of line you let out and how much bait you will accept on the hook or lure. Don't let the credit card company have control of the fishing pole! It's your pole so take ownership of it, and that involves responsibility and strict discipline. If successful at this, you will enjoy fishing; but if not, get used to the snags, near catches and the ones that got away because you will not enjoy your fishing experience.

The worst case scenario is when the fishing line breaks. If you get to this stage, then you are in serious trouble because you don't have the ability or available resources to pay back the credit card debt. Bankruptcy may be the next alternative. As stated, get control of the fishing pole of credit cards. Let out only the line you really need and be careful how much bait you will accept.

Better yet, do your best to reel in the line, put the fishing pole away for awhile and only occasionally go on a short, planned and controlled fishing trip. Credit card "fishing" can be either a rewarding or a dangerous sport. Be careful.

Credit Card Features & Benefits

$ $ $

In order to encourage consumers to use their card, credit card companies attach specific features and benefits to their card which make them competitive and yet distinguishable from all the other credit cards available.

Features

You can get a basic major credit card which usually comes with a credit limit of under $5,000.00 and may or may not have an annual fee attached. Or, other features of a gold credit card, such as travel benefits, collision damage waiver protection or out-of-province and country medical insurance, may make paying the annual fee worth it to you. In the credit card marketplace, there are also USD denominated major credit cards available.

Department store and gas station credit cards are surging ahead with their own credit card features in an attempt to get their card not only in your wallet or purse, but in your hand being used. As time goes on, you will see more joint credit card ventures between two or more retailers with some sort of bonus program attached. There are also "affinity" cards. Some Canadian universities and colleges will offer a credit card through a major credit card company. Every transaction you do may give the school a small fee paid by the credit card issuer and not the user. The more cards used, the higher the fees paid to the school as revenue which in turn may lower tuition costs.

Benefits

Benefits are add-ons to make one credit card look more attractive than another credit card to the consumer. One major credit card may attempt to sway you by guaranteeing that they will always offer the best interest rate of all credit cards. Others may offer miles for traveling, merchandise, discounts or money towards the purchase of your first home. The benefits shouldn't be the only thing that sways you to use one credit card company over another.

Annual Fees

When deciding which credit card is best for you, the annual fee should also be considered. Make sure you are receiving the value of the features and benefits of a credit card in comparison to the annual fee cost. One major credit card may offer you a lower interest rate, but if you don't keep a balance or a very small balance, does the annual fee for this credit card really save you any money? This is something to evaluate and compare when researching credit cards.

The Real Reason

The item that should sway you the most is the interest rate charged. The real reason all credit card issuers want to attract you to their card is because most people carry a balance on their card and, therefore, interest charges collected can be very profitable to the credit card company. Some of the card's features are paid for by an annual card fee while other "benefits" to the cardholder are easily absorbed as an expense by the credit card company because they more than make it back with the interest collected. This is why each credit card issuer is trying to attract you away from the credit card company you normally use. And, the company you normally use is changing the features on their card to ensure that you stay with them. A lot of market research is done by credit card companies as they seek to have the upper edge in a world filled with wants and greed.

As discussed in the chapter on credit card risks, be very careful that you are not lured into obtaining too many credit cards. You need to study what features would benefit you the most. If travel benefits are important to you, then research and compare what one card offers in comparison to another card. Every FI and other credit card issuer will have pamphlets about their credit cards which will provide you with all the information you need. Of course, the FI with which you do your banking will strongly suggest that since you do your regular banking with them, it would be much easier for you to have one of their credit cards. This is true to an extent, although with the increase of telephone banking, you can often make payments to a variety of different credit card companies and not even step into your FI's branch. Therefore, convenience is not really a factor.

Research the features and benefits that you need the most in order to minimize the number of credit cards you carry – that is the key.

Personal Loans

$ $ $

There are a variety of reasons for requesting a personal loan. You could be purchasing a vehicle, consolidating your debts, going on a holiday, purchasing furniture or appliances, making home renovations, etc. There are also a variety of places where you can apply for this loan. Many retailers will have their internal connections which they will try to persuade you to use. For example, many furniture stores have financing available through a small loans company. The car dealers will have connections with larger FI's.

Banks, trust companies and credit unions all do personal loans. However, the policies at one FI may be very different than those at another FI. This means that if one FI can't do the loan for you, another FI may consider it since their lending policies are different. Be careful how many places you go looking for a personal loan, or credit of any kind, for that matter. Every time you apply for credit, your credit bureau is pulled. Every FI that pulls your credit bureau will show the date they obtained your credit bureau. It is viewed that if you have 3-6 of these within a six-month period, you could be considered a credit seeker and, therefore, be declined your loan request based on that fact alone. Therefore, research policy information before you apply for a loan. Only when you are actually ready to have the application taken should you proceed, because then that FI will pull your credit bureau automatically.

Small Loans Companies

If you decide to go through a small loans company, be prepared to pay a higher interest rate than what you should be able to receive at your FI. On the other hand, some FI's will not consider loans under a specific dollar amount unless a higher interest rate than the rate for other personal loans is charged or if you apply for or use their credit card product.

Loan Types

Most personal loans are classified as "unsecured lending." Even though your FI takes a vehicle, RV or boat as collateral on a loan, it is still called unsecured lending. If a vehicle is taken as collateral, the loan may be referred to as a chattel term loan, but it is also still an unsecured loan. Secured lending means the FI is taking cash, term deposits, mutual funds or real estate as collateral. A specific time frame for repayment, or a term, is established when the loan is granted. This is why the phrase "term loans" is also used in place of "unsecured lending."

There are also interest only demand loans which are used under special circumstances. If a person needs interim financing between the date of the purchase and the sale of a house, they may require short term interim financing which will usually be set up as a demand loan requiring interest only payments. Demand loans are usually short term in nature and are not commonly used in personal lending.

As mentioned in the RSP section of this book, you can also take out an RSP loan for the sole purpose of purchasing an RSP to invest at the FI from which you took the loan. For more details about this, please look up this information in the "Investments" section.

Loan Term Types

Each FI or small loans company will offer you a couple of choices regarding the term of your interest rate. A variable rate term loan means that for the life of the whole loan, your interest rate will rise and fall with prime rate or a specified base interest rate used by the FI. This is great when interest rates fall because the loan is costing you less money over time. However, if interest rates rise, you will also see your payment go up which means you are paying more in interest for this loan than when you first took out the loan. A renewable rate term loan means that for the specified term, usually 6 months to a year, you will be guaranteed a specific interest rate for that time frame whether interest rates go up or down. When the term is up, the loan will automatically renew for another similar term at the current interest rate on the date of renewal. If your payment changes, you will usually be sent a notice. The final one is a fixed rate term loan. This means that for the whole term of the loan, usually up to five years maximum, you are locked into a specific interest rate whether the other rates go up or down. If you want to know that your payments will never change or if interest rates are on the rise, this is the term loan you need.

Repayment Terms

As stated, usually you cannot go over five years to repay your loan. The FI may tell you the maximum time frame you will be allowed or they may leave this up to you to choose. For very large purchases, such as boats, RV's, airplanes, mobile homes and luxury vehicles, the FI may have a policy that allows you a longer time frame of repayment in order to make the payments reasonable. Again, this is a policy set by each individual FI.

Loan Conditions

Most personal loans are open. This means that you can pay any extra amount you want on the loan at any time without a penalty. In fact, you can pay off the loan in full at any time. Another feature is that you are allowed to increase your payment at any time. This results in more money going towards principal reduction of your loan. In both scenarios, you will end up paying less in interest charges and have the loan paid off faster.

Some FI's allow flexibility in repayment frequency. Instead of only monthly payments, you may be allowed to choose weekly, bi-weekly or semi-monthly. My suggestion is to set up your payment date on the same day you are paid, both for ease of budgeting and so that the loan is paid off more quickly. Of course, your FI may only have monthly payments which will make this suggestion more difficult unless you are paid monthly.

Loan Extensions

On an exception basis, your FI may let you "extend" or "skip" a loan payment if necessary. This means that you will be allowed to miss the upcoming payment of both principal and interest. It doesn't mean that you never have to make up the loan payment. Depending on what type of loan you have, normally this payment will be added to the end of the loan repayment time. By doing this extension, your loan will end up costing you more money in interest charges since the principal wasn't reduced when it was supposed to be reduced. Only request an extension if you really have to. Often for the FI's better loan customers, they will offer you a loan extension, usually around Christmas or in January when cash flows are often very tight. If you accept their offer, then you are also accepting the fact that this loan will end up costing you more in the end and it will take that extra time to pay it off in full.

Interest Rate Negotiations

Your loan interest rate is often less negotiable than a mortgage interest rate. Quite often, the FI will set the interest rate and, unless you have a large portfolio with them, they are not likely to budge on the interest rate charged. As a consumer, you are free to research interest rates from one FI to another; however, your FI may not be able to match another FI's interest rate, which leaves you with a decision to make about which FI you want to do the loan through. The lowest interest rate isn't necessarily the best place to take out your loan if it isn't your regular FI. You have to evaluate any extra administration you will have in getting the payments to the other FI on time, etc. If possible, see if they can charge your bank account at your FI instead as this is a possibility at some FI's. Then the lowest interest rate makes the most sense because you don't have to administer more than one bank account at more than one FI.

Loans and Budgeting

As with credit card debts, you must budget for any loan payments. Before you walk in to the loans officer's office, you should know from your budget worksheet what you can afford for payments. It makes sense to be well prepared ahead of time instead of worrying afterwards if you can really afford the loan payment.

Car Dealership Loans/Leasing

$ $ $

When you look for your vehicle at a car dealership, the salesman and business manager will talk with you about financing the vehicle. If it is a brand new vehicle, you will often be given three different choices:

Purchase & Finance Through Car Company's Credit Division

This means that you will buy and own the vehicle. The loan will be arranged through the credit division of the same company that sold you the vehicle. The large car manufacturers have their own internal finance companies. Sometimes you can obtain lower interest rates than at an FI this way because the car manufacturer is trying to help their dealerships sell off inventory more easily. This usually happens when the manufacturer has too many vehicles in their inventory back at the factory and needs to stimulate interest in the marketplace to sell this vehicle. So, it really helps both the car dealership and the car manufacturer to offer lower interest rates internally in order to get the vehicle sold and off the dealership's lot. Of course, the consumer can benefit from this also, but only if the lower interest rate is offered on the vehicle you want to purchase. You may find that only a select vehicle name is being offered with a low interest rate or cash back. This means that this vehicle may not be selling as well as the manufacturer would like. Therefore, they create a good reason for a person to purchase that vehicle.

Purchase and Finance Through a Financial Institution

Notice it says "a Financial Institution." You should talk with your FI before you go car shopping. Find out the best interest rate and terms they will offer you. When you get to the dealership, the salesperson will be interested in how you plan to pay for the vehicle. That is when you will usually talk with the business manager. This person will let you know all about the best interest rates available and which FI is offering them. You may inquire about your own FI and discover one of two things. Either your FI isn't involved in "dealer finance loans" or the interest rate offered at the dealership is less than that offered at the FI's branch. A dealer finance loan means a special arrangement is made between the dealership and the FI to offer potential vehicle purchasers financing arranged at the dealership instead of going into an FI's branch. Often these dealer finance loans offer lower interest rates than if you walked into your FI. Again, you have to evaluate everything that is offered and make the best decision. As far as your payment is concerned, if you bank with Bank A and the loan is arranged through Bank B, then through a dealer finance loan you can have Bank B take your loan payment from your Bank A account. Of course, Bank B would like you to bring all your banking to them and Bank A really won't like it that you have your loan at Bank B. However, you have to do whatever is best for you.

Lease Finance Through the Dealership

Basically, a lease means that you are renting the vehicle from the car company for a specific time frame at a specific payment amount. Your down payment and regular payments are helping to cover the depreciation and interest costs that occur on the vehicle for the life of the lease. That way when you return the vehicle after the lease expires, the car dealership will be able to sell the used vehicle and not lose out since you have paid the depreciation up to that point in time plus interest costs.

As you can tell, you don't own the vehicle. Instead, when the lease expires, there is usually a buy back clause that will allow you the opportunity to purchase the vehicle outright from the car company for a specified amount of money. If you don't proceed to purchase, then you will hand in the keys to the dealership. You could still owe some money on the vehicle depending on what shape you return the vehicle in after the lease has expired. Any wear and tear beyond normal conditions may be your responsibility. This will be written in your lease agreement, so read it carefully.

Leasing instead of owning has grown in popularity. Often, the lease payments will be less than the loan payment option; however, by leasing you don't own the vehicle, so it is not an asset of yours. There are professions that will tend to lease instead of owning a vehicle. It is important to them to be driving a newer vehicle either for comfort or for status reasons. After the lease is over, the vehicle is returned and they select another vehicle with another lease. These professions or people only need the new vehicle for a short term. If you plan on keeping the vehicle for the long term (over 5 years), then a loan, or owning the vehicle, may be the best alternative.

If you are purchasing and taking out a loan or leasing, read the paperwork very carefully and don't be afraid to ask questions.

Personal Line of Credit

$ $ $

There are two line of credit types available. One is called an unsecured line of credit and the other a secured line of credit. Before explanation is given as to what the differences are, let's take a brief look at the features of a line of credit.

If approved, you are given a limit, or a line, up to which you are allowed to borrow, or a credit limit. If your approved limit is $20,000.00, then you can borrow up to that maximum number, but you don't have to borrow the whole limit at once. You can use $5,000.00 of it now, or nothing at all, and leave the remaining allowable limit for future use. If you use $5,000.00 now, then you are paying interest on this amount that you have drawn out of the line. The other $15,000.00 allowable limit is not being used and, therefore, you don't pay any interest on it.

The beauty of the line of credit is that unlike a loan:

1. You control how much line you need at any given time;
2. If you don't use the whole line immediately, you still have it for future use to pay off or draw on when you need;
3. When you have paid the line down to a zero balance, it isn't closed like a loan, but is still open and available for future use.

It is a very flexible lending product. Often your minimum payment is either interest only or a specific percent of the previous month's outstanding balance, usually 3-5% payment. With a loan, on the other hand, you have fixed payments even though your balance is decreasing. Most lines of credit (LOC) fluctuate as a variable rate loan would. If prime rate goes up or down, the interest rate charged will also go up or down accordingly. However, it is cheaper than a credit card interest rate.

So, you can arrange an LOC and not even use it right away. It is available to use when you need it and more flexible than other types of credit products. It is not a product for everyone. Just like credit cards, you have been given a limit which you must live within and be able to pay back in a timely manner. If you have any difficulties with a credit card, then this is not a credit product I would suggest for you.

Unsecured LOC

If you reflect back to the chapter on loans, unsecured means that there is no actual security against the loan or LOC except your signature. No collateral at all is taken on an unsecured personal LOC. You will pay a higher interest rate than if it was a secured LOC. But on the other side, you will usually pay less on an unsecured LOC than you would on an unsecured loan.

Secured LOC

There are three methods used to secure an LOC. The first two are by either providing cash collateral or a term deposit/mutual fund/money market instrument as collateral, either dollar for dollar or at a margined ratio depending on what the actual securities consist of. The third method is by way of a first or second mortgage against your house. This means that you are having a mortgage registered against your principal residence. You are using the equity in your home to provide collateral against the LOC. You must make sure the costs to put this together are worth the benefits of the lower interest rate required. In other words, a $10,000.00 secured LOC as a mortgage may not be worth your while due to the costs involved in setting it up (appraisal, legal, etc.).

The main benefit of a secured LOC is that you will be required to pay a lower rate of interest than the unsecured LOC. As stated, just make sure the benefits outweigh the costs.

The following example is getting a bit ahead of ourselves, but LOC's secured by a mortgage fits better in this section than in the mortgage section. Usually when setting up an LOC mortgage, the maximum loan to value the FI will consider is 75% of the appraised value with both the 1st and 2nd mortgages added together. That sentence is a mouth full, so let me explain in detail.

Example: Line of Credit as a Mortgage

Appraised House Value	$150,000.00
Current 1st Mortgage Balance	$85,000.00
Equation:	
Calculate 75% of Appraised Value	
$150,000.00 x 75%	$112,500.00
Subtract 1st Mortgage Balance	$85,000.00
Equals Maximum 2nd Mortgage LOC =	$27,500.00

Of course, you still have to qualify for this LOC based on your income and credit history. Rarely will any major FI put a 3rd or greater mortgage on your principal residence as an LOC. If your 1st mortgage is at Bank A and you are arranging the 2nd mortgage LOC at Bank B, the above equation may have a few adjustments.

Co-Signor's Responsibility

$ $ $

Many people don't understand or realize that when you co-sign on another person's debt you are as responsible for that debt as they are. You may think that you are only somewhat responsible if payments are not made since the other person you are co-signing for is gaining from the loan in the first place. However, this isn't the case. If the loan goes into any kind of delinquency, whether you know about this delinquency or not, it may reflect on your credit bureau also. If payments are not made, you will be called upon to make up any past due payments plus future payments "as if you were the person you co-signed for." When you sign the loan, you are not 50% responsible you are 100% responsible. Why do I keep stressing this? Because people are either misinformed or don't listen when advice is being given about co-signing on another person's debt. I have seen some very stressful cases in my career where the co-signor is called upon, but he is not prepared for the extra payments and it then ruins his good credit rating also. If you are going to co-sign, go into it with both eyes open. This extra payment, which hopefully you will never have to make, should be budgeted for just in case.

A lot of parents co-sign for sons or daughters to help them obtain credit. It is good to teach this kind of responsibility, but realize that it is also your credit rating that is at risk here. You have a responsibility to ensure that payments are made on time, as does your child. More and more parents are co-signing on mortgages for their children. Realize that this could be a lengthy time commitment since a mortgage can be amortized over 25 years. If the FI doesn't feel comfortable taking you off the mortgage as a co-signor, they don't have to release you from this responsibility.

If you are considering co-signing for a friend or relative, consider that the FI wouldn't lend to this person in the first place. So, if they accept you as a co-signor, then you are the strength of the deal which means that if they don't pay, the FI believes you will. You are the collateral on the loan. Whether a vehicle is taken as collateral or not, you are the real collateral on the loan.

So, make sure you fully understand what your responsibilities are as a co-signor before you sign on the line. There is a serious measure of risk here that you may not be comfortable with. Use the wisdom God has given you. Also, take the emotion out of the decision if you can.

What Happens If I Don't Pay?

$ $ $

Throughout this section on borrowing money, I have been persistent about being very careful with debt and making sure it fits within your budget. Of course, life has its earthly uncertainties at times. Career changes, job loss, going back to school to upgrade skills, pay reductions due to cutbacks and strikes, to name a few, can affect how you are going to pay your bills, whether you have a budget or not. You see, the budget is only good for the immediate. Hopefully, built into it is a savings category for the future uncertainties; however, your budget's main concern is to get you from one paycheque to the next in a disciplined manner.

The current economy will dictate how much money you should store away in case any of these or other misfortunes happen. If unemployment is high, it means to get back into the workforce may take some time. Therefore, having 3 month's wages saved away may not get you through. Don't depend on UIC benefits to carry you through these times. You may have to dip into your RSP savings in order to make ends meet. This isn't what they were meant for, but when there is nowhere else to turn, you may have to sacrifice the long term gains the RSP was providing you with in order to satisfy the short term money squeeze.

If you don't pay your creditor, several things can happen. The credit company will usually start by phoning you constantly. Only promise them what you know you can do. One thing that gets collectors really upset is when you promise something and don't come through as you said you would. Believe it or not, you have to build some trust with the collector. However, the one time you don't come through as promised, they may pull the plug on you. Some collectors can be very difficult to work with. Their job is to get the debt collected immediately, under almost any circumstances and using almost any methods. Try to be reasonable. However, if the collector won't listen to you rationally, request to talk to their supervisor or phone back and ask to talk to their supervisor. Of course, sometimes this can cause more friction between you and the person assigned your file as it will be viewed as you trying to go above their head. Be careful and use wisdom.

At all times, the lateness of the debt payment will be reported to the credit bureau. This will cause you problems in the future if you are seeking credit even if you have paid this problem debt off in full. The history of any previous late payment(s) will be on your credit bureau for 7 years.

The uncollected debt could be assigned to a collection agency if the creditor is unsuccessful in its attempt to collect. These agencies get paid a commission on the dollar amount they collect. Therefore, they really want to collect the debt. They will be very aggressive in their approach almost to the point of being offensive. All I can say is do what you can to keep yourself from being mixed up with the collection agency.

The creditor may seek a judgment against you through the courts and attach this judgment to an asset of yours. Usually, this will be done if they discover that you are a homeowner. A lien or judgment can be put against your house so that if you ever sell the house, they will be paid. This can be expensive for the creditor to do, so on small unpaid debts, it is unlikely that this course of action will be taken.

Another possibility is to obtain court approval to garnishee your wages if the creditor discovers that you are employed. This will have a great effect on your budgeting because they don't just take small amounts of money off each paycheque to be put towards this debt; you could see large amounts taken off your paycheque for a number of paycheques until the debt is paid in full.

Ultimately, if you don't pay your debts and you have no assets worth selling, you can declare personal bankruptcy. The law permits you to start with a clean slate again with your creditors being forced to write off the debt as a bad debt or unrecoverable loss if they were not holding security on the loan. If you go bankrupt, you will have a long and laborious journey to obtain credit again for some time because the bankruptcy will show on your credit bureau. Most lenders are very leery about lending to a previous bankrupt. The bankruptcy may have got the past creditors off your case, but it will hinder your ability to obtain new credit in the future.

There could be other methods used to collect on past due accounts. If the FI took your car as collateral against the loan, they may send out the bailiff to collect the car and sell it off to receive some of the loan's balance back. If you have a mortgage and don't keep up on the payments, then the mortgagor has the option to foreclose on you through the courts, sell the house and gain back the amount owed plus all the expenses they incurred to complete the foreclosure, which usually leaves nothing left over.

Make sure you are not in too much debt at any given time in case the unexpected happens and you are out of work tomorrow or whatever the case may be. Plan ahead and be careful about any extra debt load.

Life & Disability Insurance

$ $ $

Whether you are applying for a loan, line of credit or a mortgage, the topic of insurance will come into the discussion at some time.

Loans

Most loans offer life and disability insurance. The life insurance will pay out the loan's balance in full if you die, which means your estate won't have to be concerned with it. Often you can have up to two people life insured on the loan if two of you are borrowers on the loan. The insurance premium is based on the age of the borrower(s) at the time the loan is taken out and the amount of money originally borrowed. There is usually a health question that you have to answer. Depending on your answer, you could be life insured immediately. You must be honest in answering this question because if you answer falsely and you do die, the loan will not be covered by the insurance company.

The disability insurance can come in different packages. Depending on where you borrow the money for the loan, you may be offered disability insurance that will take effect 7 days, 14 days or 30 days after the disability happens. The cost of the disability insurance depends on how soon it will take effect and the amount of money borrowed. The more expensive choice will be the option that takes effect 7 days after a disability. Now, the disability doesn't have to happen at work. You could be crossing the road and you get hit by a car and can't work due to the injury. Or, you could be skiing and have an unfortunate accident on the slopes. The disability insurance covers the loan payment while you are off work. You will have forms to complete with both your employer and your doctor. The insurance coverage will continue as long as the claim is accepted by the insurance company as a legitimate claim.

How the insurance premiums are collected from you may be different from one FI to another or from an FI to a car dealership. One method is to collect the insurance premiums as part of the loan payment. You pay as you go. Your payment will consist of Principal + Interest + Life Insurance (if taken) + Disability Insurance (if taken). If you pay the loan out early, then you have only paid insurance up to the point in time when the loan is paid in full. The other method, which is used by the car dealerships mostly, is to charge for the whole life insurance and/or disability insurance up front. This could calculate into hundreds of dollars. Since most of us don't have this kind of money up front, the insurance premium will be added to the loan and you will pay it back with interest over the life of the loan. If you pay the car dealership loan off early, you must remember to request an insurance rebate form from the car dealership. If you don't request a rebate on the insurance, then you have really overpaid and the insurance company will usually pocket the overpayment. Therefore, be certain you receive back what you are due.

Personal Line of Credit

You will find that most offer life insurance on the line of credit, but few offer disability insurance. The life insurance is paid on the amount outstanding based on your age now instead of when you originally took out the LOC. Therefore, the premiums paid can go up over time since the LOC balance can fluctuate up and down over time. As an example, the year you took out the LOC you were 30 years old and today you are 33. If 33 puts you into the next premium bracket, then your life insurance payable will also go up. As you can see, you pay as you go on whatever is currently outstanding. If your limit is $20,000.00 and you have a current balance of $9,000.00, then you will only pay the life insurance premium on the outstanding balance of $9,000.00.

Now, if you were diagnosed with a life-threatening disease and your limit was $20,000.00 and your balance owing was at $9,000.00, you could be tempted to spend money until you are at your limit because the LOC is life insured. Be careful here because most LOC life insurance applications have a disclaimer clause that will only cover up to the amount owing at the time of the diagnosis of the life threatening disease. If you do put the LOC to the limit after the diagnosis and die, then your estate will be faced with paying off the difference between the balance at death and the amount that was owing when the diagnosis occurred. This is very important to be aware of because there are some very large LOC's out there which could mean very large unpaid balances for the estate to manage if this scenario occurs.

If disability insurance is offered, you will usually pay a monthly premium on the outstanding balance. If you get injured and are off work for the minimum time frame required, the disability insurance will only be paid on the balance owing at the time which the disability took place. So, don't think that just because you have a disability claim, you can rack the LOC to the limit because the insurance company will pay for it. This is not the case, so be wise and careful.

Mortgages

Some mortgages offer life, disability and loss of work insurance. The latter two types of insurance are very expensive, but might be worth your while. When considering insurance on your mortgage, you need to be very careful about which insurance you take to ensure that it suits your needs. A mortgage is usually a lot of money so you want to ensure that you are covered adequately. The premium you pay will depend on your age and the age of the second person on the mortgage, if this is the case, and the amount of the mortgage when you first borrow the money. The premium will not change throughout the mortgage unless you re-mortgage the house, which means that you take out a new mortgage. Therefore, unlike an LOC, an increase in age does not mean an increase in the premiums payable. However, also unlike an LOC, as the balance goes down, your premiums stay the same as if you were still borrowing the original amount.

Some people think it is better to approach an insurance agent and take the life insurance out through them instead. In some cases, this may prove to be a better choice; however, what this really requires is your time and effort to research both options and determine what is best for you. If you walk into the FI to sign the mortgage paperwork and haven't done your research, then I would suggest you take the insurance offered by the FI and proceed to research after the fact because you can always cancel your insurance at the FI later. However, if you decide not to take the FI's life insurance and later discover that you should have, you will have to go through a lengthy process to prove that you are eligible for the life insurance after the fact. So, if you are uncertain, take the FI's life insurance now and research afterwards.

As stated, the disability insurance and loss of work insurance are very costly to you, so you had better need this insurance if you are going to pay for it. Again, consider researching this through a life insurance agent.

Most people don't like talking about insurance because if you ever make a claim, it usually means something bad has happened. However, if you have a family to support, then you should be giving consideration to their needs if you were to die unexpectedly. Make sure you have adequate insurance to cover your debts to ensure that your loved ones are cared for if something happens to you or to your spouse.

Summary of Borrowing Money – Personal Lending

$ $ $

- Respect debt. Get a handle on your debt load before it takes control of you. Be disciplined about both saving, spending and borrowing money.

- As Christians, we are here to do God's will on earth and not to simply satisfy our own cravings and desires.

- The credit interview can be somewhat unnerving, but now that you are familiar with both what happens during the interview and what is expected from you, this should ease any concerns you have.

- By completing the Credit Application Worksheet, you will be very familiar with the questions the lending officer will be asking and the information you need to provide.

- There are very serious risks to credit card debt. Be certain who is holding the fishing pole in your life when it comes to your credit card debt(s).

- Most credit cards come with various features and benefits attached. Be sure you research which card(s) is/are best for you in order to minimize the number of cards used.

- There is a lot to know about personal loans. Be sure you understand how your loan operates, its type and the terms and conditions.

- If you are purchasing a vehicle through a car dealership, be aware of what the differences are between a loan arranged at your FI compared to one arranged at the car dealership.

- Personal line of credit is a very flexible lending product which isn't for everyone. There are benefits to a secured LOC, but make sure the benefits outweigh the expense involved in setting up a secured LOC if you choose this route.

- You must realize that budgeting is an integral part of your personal finances that must not be forgotten when looking to set up any loan facility. If your budget says you can't afford the loan, then you had better not be borrowing money.

- If you don't or can't pay your debts, there are various results that could occur. Try your best to plan ahead for uncertainties in life.

- When setting up a personal borrowing product, discussion will come up about various types of insurance that are available to protect you and your family. This is important, so be prepared to research, if necessary, for what is best for you and your family.

Borrowing Money – Mortgages

$ $ $

The Scripture verses below don't have a lot to do with mortgages. However, Jesus' parable shows the difference between being wise and not being wise. A house is considered the largest dollar purchase item most people make in life and their mortgage is usually the largest debt the average person incurs. For these reasons, it is vitally important that you study, understand and gain wisdom when it comes to your personal mortgage.

"Therefore everyone who hears these words of mine and puts them into practice is like a wise man who built his house on the rock. The rain came down, the streams rose, and the winds blew and beat against that house; yet it did not fall, because it had its foundation on the rock. But everyone who hears these words of mine and does not put them into practice is like a foolish man who built his house on sand. The rain came down, the streams rose, and the winds blew and beat against that house, and it fell with a great crash."

Matthew 7:24-27

Mortgage Application Process

$ $ $

You have been driving around looking at all the houses that have "For Sale" signs on them and matching them to the weekly Real Estate paper to see what features are in the house for what price. You have an idea of what you would like, but you aren't sure if you can afford it or not. You already have a Realtor chosen (unless you are purchasing a privately listed house) that you want to approach. Most times, the first question the Realtor may ask you is, "Have you been to your Financial Institution to see what amount of mortgage you can be pre-approved to?" Before they spend time with you looking at houses, they want to know that the houses they are showing you fit within your budget. So, this is where an appointment with your FI's lending officer or mortgage broker will have to happen.

The pre-approval will be given based on the fact that the information given to the lender is accurate and true. Most pre-approvals will not require you to prove your income at that time, but when you do need to prove your income and it isn't what you originally said it was, then this will change the amount you will be allowed to borrow, which means your pre-approval from before will have to be altered. The pre-approval will be subject to your income verification, credit bureau review, down payment confirmation, appraisal and possibly the mortgage insurer's approval (if the insurer is needed). You will leave knowing the amount of mortgage you are preapproved to, plus your down payment, equaling the price range you can look at in housing. In the section on "Borrowing Money – Personal Lending," there was a blank credit application provided. Have this completed before going to the mortgage pre-approval interview.

Once you have found the house you want to purchase, your Realtor will write up a contract of purchase which is your offer to the people selling the house, the vendors. Advice as to what to put in this contract is what the Realtor is being paid for. If for any reason you are unsure of the legal ramifications of the contract, you could take it to your lawyer or notary to have it explained to you before you sign it. Of course, this will cost you extra in fees, but when purchasing a large ticket item like a house you had better know what you are signing. Once signed, this will be presented to the vendor who may want to make changes to your offer, which means they are counter-offering. This could go back and forth for a while, although it usually only counter offers back and forth a few times until a final agreement can be reached. Once an agreement is reached, you will need to give your Realtor a deposit of a specific amount of money that binds the contract and is agreed to in the contract. This money will eventually go to your lawyer/notary and form part of the down payment you need to give them later anyways.

Make sure, even if you are pre-approved, that you put a subject to financing clause in the purchase contract. As stated, the pre-approval is an indication of what you will be approved for, but it is not the final word since the house will need to be appraised, etc.

You will take this legal contract to your FI or broker along with whatever other information the FI or broker needs and wait for a reply back from them. If the reply is favourable, which means you are approved, then the Realtor will arrange to remove subjects which, when removed, legally bind you to purchase the house on the closing date.

From here you will usually attend the FI again to sign various paperwork and go over the terms and conditions of your mortgage one more time. The FI will arrange for the legal paperwork to be sent to the lawyer or notary you have chosen. You should be arranging your fire insurance coverage at this time. Your lawyer/notary will need to know where this fire insurance has been arranged. The lawyer/notary will prepare the legal mortgage documentation and have you attend their office for signing. They should provide you with explanations as to what you are signing and answer any questions you may have relating to the mortgage. They will usually tell you ahead of your visit what amount of money you need to bring with you to cover the down payment plus the costs involved. The legal office will then arrange the payment of money to the vendor on the closing date.

As of the closing date, the house keys will be given to you and you now own the house – congratulations! Now you just have to move into the house and set it up as you had previously dreamed when you first looked at the house.

How Do I Calculate Mortgage Payments?

$ $ $

Before computers, bankers used various charts to figure out what payments would be on a mortgage. Each chart would be for a different amortization period with the interest rates all listed by increments of 1/8% along the top and amounts of money borrowed listed along the side. You can still purchase such charts at a book or stationery store. However, with computers, these books have become obsolete. Due to my completing the mortgage brokers course, I often use my special calculator to work out payments. This is a very helpful tool, especially when the computer system isn't working properly.

If you own your own personal computer, there are programs available which will not only calculate a mortgage payment, but also give you a full amortization schedule. You can create and print off various "what if" scenarios for yourself. Be sure you use "compounding semi-annually interest rate, not in advance" when inputting the interest rate type.

If you don't have access to a personal computer that has this type of program, then approach your FI as they will have programs on their computers which can print out various scenarios for you to keep. Of course, if you do approach your FI, they may want to follow up with you and even pre-approve you while you are in their office. If you are ready for this, then great. If you aren't, then arrange for a more appropriate time that is suitable to you.

In this book, it would be too difficult to provide you with a mortgage scenario for every mortgage amount at every interest rate with different amortizations. Unfortunately, the calculation of a mortgage payment is not a simple equation. However, when you input the information into a computer it seems very simple.

What Is GDSR & TDSR?

$ $ $

To really get a lot out of this chapter, it is helpful if you have access to a personal computer that can calculate mortgage payments. If you don't, the information is still very useful and worth reading to obtain an understanding of how these ratios are calculated, but you won't be able to get any hands-on experience unless you want to use fictitious numbers for the mortgage payments.

Your FI will calculate these two ratios to determine if your income level fits within both your mortgage debt and the total of all your debts. This is provided here to give you an idea of what they look at, so you can go into the interview better educated.

GDSR

These initials stand for Gross Debt Service Ratio. The maximum GDSR allowed is usually between 30-32%.

TDSR

These initials stand for Total Debt Service Ratio. The maximum TDSR allowed is usually between 40-42%.

In the worksheet below, it is assumed that this is a conventional mortgage. If you are doing an insured mortgage, then the payments on the mortgage will be slightly higher. However, for ease of calculation, we won't get into these other particulars here.

THE ABC'S OF DEBT SERVICE RATIO CALCULATION WORKSHEET

STEP 1: What Is the Total Income Being Used?

Turn into annualized income (therefore, if paid monthly, multiply by 12, if bi-weekly multiply by 26, etc.)

Applicant #1 income = $_____ x _____ = $_____ /year
Applicant #2 income = $_____ x _____ = $_____ /year

Total annualized income   = $_____ /year **(A)**

STEP 2: What Is the Total Mortgage Amount Going To Be?

Purchase Price of House $_____ **(B)**
Less: Down payment $_____
Equals Mortgage Amount of $_____ **(C)**

STEP 3: What Is the Loan To Lending Value Ratio?

Take **(B)** above and divide it by **(C)** above: _____ / _____ = _____ %
                                                    (B)   **(C)**   **(D)**

STEP 4: What Are Mortgage Payments On This?

Go to your personal computer and input the amount of mortgage, amortization, interest rate, term, if asked, and ensure that the interest rate compounds semi-annually not in advance (or # compound frequencies = 2). Use the monthly payment in our calculations even if you plan on paying bi-weekly, etc.

Write here what your monthly mortgage payment will be _____ and multiply it by 12 to get an annualized mortgage payment = _____ **(E)**

STEP 5: What Is the Gross Debt Service Ratio (GDSR)?

Add Together:

1) the annualized mortgage payment found in **(E)**	$_____
2) the annualized property taxes	$_____
3) the space heating costs (usually $900/year)	$_____
4) 1/2 of condo or maintenance fee	$_____

Total $_____ **(F)**

Write down the total annualized income as found in **(A)** above $_____

(A)

Divide **(F)** by **(A)** to get the GDSR % _____ / _____ = ____ %

(F)   **(A)**   **(G)**

STEP 6: What Is the Total Debt Service Ratio (TDSR)?

Annualize all of your other monthly debts including loan payments, LOC payments and credit card payments.

Item:

_____	$_____
_____	$_____
_____	$_____
_____	$_____
_____	$_____
_____	$_____
_____	$_____
Total of all other annualized debt	$_____ **(H)**
Add to **(H)** the total found in **(F)**	$_____ **(F)**
This gives you total of all debts	$_____ **(J)**

Now divide **(J)** by **(A)** to get the TDSR: _____ / _____ = _____ %

(K)   **(J)**   **(A)**

STEP 7: Now Does It Fit?

GDSR = _____ (G)
TDSR = _____ (K)

Further Notes:

Amortization & Term

$ $ $

To understand your mortgage and how it operates, you need to fully understand what is meant by amortization and term.

Amortization

Amortization is the whole length of your mortgage from beginning to end. Usually the maximum allowed is 25 years amortization. That means the mortgage is stretched over this time frame to allow for reduced payments to make the mortgage payment bearable. The longer the amortization, the lower the payment amount will become. This may help your cashflow; however, the longer the amortization, the less of each payment is going towards your principal reduction of the mortgage. Let's give an example here. The mortgage amount is $150,000.00 and the interest rate is 7.50%.

If you put this over a 25-year amortization, your payment will be $1,097.33/month. Of the first payment, $923.18 will go towards interest and $174.15 will be applied towards the principal. In five years, your balance owing, if all payments were made on time, will be $137,406.65.

If you were to put this same mortgage over a 20-year amortization, your payment will be $1,197.90/month. Of the first payment, $923.18 will go towards interest and $274.72 will be applied towards principal reduction. In five years, your balance owing, if all payments were made on time, will be $130,134.21.

Now put this same mortgage over a 15-year amortization and your payment will be $1,380.77/month. Of the first payment, $923.18 will go towards interest and $457.59 will be applied towards principal reduction. In five years, your balance owing, if all payments were made on time, will be $116,910.76.

163

So, you can see how shortening the amortization can save you money in the end, as long as you can afford the payment that comes with the shorter amortization.

Term

A term is the time frame you lock your mortgage in for within the amortization. You can go as short as a six-month term and as long as a 25-year term at some FI's. You are locking yourself in at a specific interest rate for this term. You will only pay that interest rate for the term chosen. So, if you take a 5-year term at 7.50%, you will pay that interest rate for the 5 years. Then, when the 5 years has expired, your mortgage will come up for renewal again and you will choose another term, which can be as short as 6 months. You will again be locked in for the time frame chosen.

Most times, the longer the term, the higher the interest rate. There have been a few times when the short term rates have been higher than the longer term rates, but this isn't common. Why is this? Think of it this way. If you were the FI, then to attract an investor to lock in for a longer term, you would need to reward them with a higher rate of interest. Since investments such as term deposits and GIC's are matched up to the FI's mortgage portfolio, then the longer term mortgage rates will need to be higher also, so that the FI can maintain its profit spread between the GIC interest rate and the mortgage interest rate.

Open Term

An open term is chosen for one of three reasons. The first is that you are unsure of which way interest rates are heading and you want total flexibility to lock in when you so desire. Being that you are open, you can do this at any time. The second reason is because you are expecting funds that you want to apply on your mortgage, but the amount is above the allowed pre-payment lump sum maximum (see separate chapter on this topic). You want to apply the money and then lock in to a specific closed term. By being open, you are allowed to do this. The last reason for going open is that you have your house on the market and hope it will sell. By being open when it does sell, you will avoid any penalties for paying off the mortgage early.

Open mortgage terms are usually 6 months or 1 year in duration. Not all FI's offer both the 6-month and 1-year options, but they will offer at least one of them.

Closed or Fixed Term

You are locking your mortgage in for a specific time frame. It can range from 6 months to 5 years or greater. Some FI's offer 7, 10 and even 25-year closed terms. The advantage is that you know what your payments are for the time frame chosen. This makes budgeting easier. The disadvantage is that if interest rates go down lower than what you locked in at you will usually have to pay a penalty in order to obtain this lower interest rate. There is more on that subject elsewhere in this book. Another disadvantage could be if you sell your house before the term is due or at renewal. Because you would be breaking the contract of your closed term early, then a penalty could be charged unless you were able to portable the mortgage to the new house you are purchasing or the person buying the house assumes your mortgage as it is from you.

Many people seem to like locking in for a closed term so that they know what their payments will be in the future. However, be content with your decision if interest rates go down lower than what you pay. The decision to lock in must be yours and not the bankers. None of us in the FI industry know exactly what interest rates are going to do either in the short term or the long term. Many customers ask our advice, which is fine, but don't expect a clear cut answer back as to what you should do. The banker doesn't want to be held responsible if they say to lock in for 5 years, and 2 years later, it appears that this wasn't the best advice, since hindsight is always 20-20. The choice is yours to make because it is your money, mortgage and debt.

Convertible Term

This is usually a closed 6-month term mortgage. It will usually offer you the lowest interest rate of all the terms available. It isn't as flexible as the open term, but it is the most flexible of all the closed terms. Convertible means you can, at any time during the 6-month term, lock your mortgage in to a closed term for 1 year or more without a fee or penalty. So, let's say you are 2 months into the 6-month term and you notice, or think, interest rates are going to go up short-ly. You have the flexibility to lock in at this 2-month mark without a fee or penalty. Why not just take the open mortgage instead? You could, but the convertible mortgage is usually at a lower interest rate than the open mortgage is; plus a fee is usually charged to lock in an open mortgage for a longer closed term, whereas the convertible usu-ally charges no extra fees.

Variable Term

A variable term means that your interest rate can fluctuate up and down during the term chosen, usually a 1-year term. Many variable terms are at prime rate. You would choose a variable term if you thought rates were going to remain steady or be going down. If rates start to rise, you are usually allowed to lock into a closed term with-out any penalty. Your payment consists of both principal and interest with a specific amortization. You are attempting to save money on your mortgage because as the interest rates go down, more of your payment will be going towards the principal of the mortgage. How-ever, if rates rise, your payment may also have to rise to make up any shortfall.

Revolving Term

This term is usually associated with a secured line of credit (LOC), which is discussed elsewhere in this section of the book. The differ-ence between this and a variable rate term is that here you are usual-ly required to pay interest only, you control the principal repayment and your minimum payment has no set amortization.

Split Term

Only a few FI's offer a split term mortgage. It means that you can have more than one, up to three usually, different terms in your same mortgage. As an example, your total mortgage may be $150,000.00.

You can set this up as:

	Amount	Time-Term	Term-Type	Amortization	Int. Rate	Paym't
Split 1	$20,000.00	6 months	Open	25 years	7.25%	$143.18
Split 2	$80,000.00	6 months	Convertible	20 years	6.50%	$592.40
Split 3	$50,000.00	5 years	Closed	15 years	8.25%	$481.06
Totals	$150,000.00					$1,216.64

Why do this? Let's say you are expecting an inheritance that you want to apply on the mortgage. You can then pay off Split 1 in full and thus reduce your payment by $143.18 without any penalty. Split 2 is set up as a convertible term so you obviously want to watch interest rates and will lock in when you want or leave as is. Split 3 means that you aren't comfortable having all of your money in a 6 month convertible term and want assurance that a specific portion is locked, or closed, for the 5 years. Notice that each split can also have its own amortization which affects the payment amount. This product is very flexible, but not for everyone.

Different Mortgage Types

$ $ $

In retail, or personal banking, there are three main types of mortgages: conventional mortgages, insured or high ratio mortgages and collateral mortgages.

Conventional Mortgages

If you are putting 25% or more as a down payment on the purchase of a home, then your FI will be putting together a conventional mortgage for you. In this case, your loan to value (LTV) is 75% (100% - 25%). There are cases where, due to the remoteness of the home and property in relation to the FI's branch, this LTV may be lower to be classified as a conventional mortgage, such as 65% or 50%. This obviously means that your down payment will have to be larger.

Insured or High Ratio Mortgages

There used to be a time when FI's couldn't mortgage more than 75% of the value of a person's home. Years ago the Federal Government changed the rules that allowed Canadians to get into their homes with less than a 25% down payment. The government created the National Housing Act which allows high ratio (above 75% LTV) mortgages. The government then created a crown corporation through which many FI's book these mortgages called Canada Mortgage and Housing Corporation (CMHC). There is also another company that will insure high ratio mortgages in Canada, but only in specific geographic markets and not anywhere in Canada. Your minimum down payment must be 10% unless you are eligible for the first time homebuyer's program which allows you to purchase with as little as a 5% down payment. The down payment must come from non-borrowed funds. It can be a gift from a relative, but a gift letter will have to be on file and proof that the relative actually has the money as the down payment will have to be presented before approval given. The gift letter will have to state that the funds are a gift and need not be repaid.

Now, you will notice that the word "insured" keeps coming up. If you are doing a high ratio mortgage, then a premium of insurance will have to be paid by you to protect the FI against the possibility of you defaulting on the mortgage. This premium varies up to 2.5% of the difference (purchase price minus the down payment) if a single advance on the mortgage, and up to 3% if more than one advance such as purchase with improvements or construction draw mortgage. The lower the LTV, the lower the premium will be.

Let's consider a $100,000.00 purchase price with a 10% down payment. This will be a single advance, which means that there is only one draw on the mortgage to complete the purchase transaction.

Purchase Price	$100,000.00
Down Payment	- $10,000.00
Difference	= $90,000.00
Insurance Premium*	+ $2,250.00
Total Mortgage Amount	$92,250.00
*($90,000 x 2.5% = $2,250)	

The FI will use the $92,250.00 when calculating your mortgage payments. You do have the option to pay this insurance premium up front, which means your mortgage would be $90,000.00, but the majority of people add this insurance premium to the mortgage. If you can afford to pay the premium up front, you will save yourself interest costs because you won't be paying interest on the premium over the amortization of the mortgage.

More than one advance means you draw a specific allowable amount of money from the approved mortgage, but not the whole amount of the mortgage. You will be doing at least one more draw at a later date. Since this adds administration to the mortgage, the premium is higher than if only one advance was made on the mortgage.

If you sell your residence and purchase another home either right away or some time in the future, you can do another high ratio mortgage (minimum 10% down payment) upon qualification from the FI. In other words, you are not restricted to the number of high ratio mortgages you can do in your lifetime, just as you can do many conventional mortgages throughout your life on different houses. However, you would not be eligible for the first time homebuyer's 5% down payment program unless unusual or extenuating circumstances occurred (see next chapter).

Collateral Mortgages

If the mortgage doesn't fit under the other two mortgage types, then the FI will consider putting together a collateral mortgage for you. Why wouldn't your mortgage "fit" the other two options? Examples would be mortgaging bare land only, house with large acreage, incomplete house, or house that doesn't meet the minimum standards due to age or condition.

Another reason is that you may need a 2nd mortgage on your house. Some FI's set these up as collateral mortgages, whereas other FI's set these up under their conventional type. As you will see in a later chapter, the disadvantage of a collateral mortgage is that it costs more in interest charges than a conventional or insured mortgage.

First Time Homebuyer – 5% Down Payment

$ $ $

Through CMHC, those who qualify are allowed to purchase their first home with as little as a 5% down payment. If there are two people purchasing the home, only one of the two has to qualify as never owning a home before. At your FI, you will sign an agreement stating that you do qualify and that will be kept in your mortgage file.

There are a few cases where you may have owned a home in the past and may still qualify for the first time homebuyer program. These are usually hardship situations or exceptions. They will require a written letter explaining your particular case, which will also be kept on file. They can include some of the following reasons:

- forced to sell previous house and move due to search for employment elsewhere in country;

- forced to sell previous house and move due to a separation or divorce;

- forced to sell house and move due to a medical reason;

- other specific reasons can be presented.

The down payment must come from non-borrowed funds. It can be a gift from a relative, but a gift letter will have to be on file and proof that the relative actually has the money as the down payment will have to be presented before approval will be given. The gift letter will have to state that the funds are a gift and need not be repaid. The insurance premium will be 2.5% if a single advance and 3% if more than one advance.

Since the Federal Government has allowed the first time homebuyer with 5% down payment program, it has provided opportunity for many Canadians to get into their first home. Previously, a minimum of 10% down payment was required whether you were a first time homebuyer or not. Just remember that the more you put down originally, the lower your payments will be and the less interest you will pay over the life of the mortgage.

Payment Frequency

$ $ $

The more often you make your mortgage payment, the quicker the mortgage balance will decrease, which means the less time it will take to pay off your mortgage. Most FI's give you a choice as to how often you want to make your mortgage payment. The choices are weekly, bi-weekly, semi-monthly and monthly. It is suggested that you match your pay period to your mortgage payment. By doing this, budgeting is made easier since your paycheque goes into your bank account and the mortgage payment immediately comes out on the same day. As you will see below, there isn't a large difference between weekly and bi-weekly payments when it comes to how soon the mortgage is paid off and the amount of interest you paid. I have seen customers who are paid bi-weekly struggle with paying weekly on their mortgage. They are constantly concerned about having enough in their account on the opposite week to their pay day, and that causes undue stress.

The following chart gives you a detailed comparison of payment frequencies. To keep things constant, this is a $100,000.00 mortgage with a 5-year term at 7.95% interest (of course, compounding semi-annually not in advance) and a 25-year amortization.

Paym't Frequency	Weekly	Bi-Weekly	Semi-Monthly	Monthly
Paym't	$189.98	$379.97	$379.97	$759.93
Term Int. Paid	$36,685.01	$36,729.87	$37,604.93	$37,696.99
Term Princ. Paid	$12,709.79	$12,666.23	$7,991.47	$7,898.81
Term End Balance	$87,290.21	$87,333.77	$92,008.53	$92,101.19
Total Years to Pay	19 yrs, 11 mos	19 yrs, 11 mos	24 yrs, 11 mos	25 yrs
Amortization Int.	$96,807.07	$97,152.60	$127,016.36	$128,183.63

Costs To Be Aware of When Purchasing & Mortgaging

$ $ $

When you purchase a house, you will need both your down payment and extra money for various closing costs associated with both the purchase and the mortgage.

Appraisal Fee

The FI may require an appraisal to be completed on the house you are purchasing. Some or all of this cost will be passed on to you. Depending on the mortgage type – conventional or insured mortgage – this cost can range from $150.00 to $235.00.

Survey Fee

A survey is a piece of paper that has a surveyor's stamp on it which guarantees for the FI what the dimensions of the property are and its shape, where the house is located within that property, whether the house is too close or over the property line or if a neighbour's house is over the property line and located on this property that is being mortgaged. In my experience, I have seen a few builders put the house in the wrong place. One such case had the corner of the person's living room actually in the golf course next door, which made mortgaging the house impossible until the property line was changed which meant paying the golf course for their land and going through lots of legal work and expense and time to complete it. Don't simply go by walking around the property and locating the surveyor's pins. These could have been moved. The actual survey from the surveyor is the official "map" of the property.

Surveys can range in price, so it is best to check with either your FI, lawyer/notary or survey company. If the vendor has a copy of the survey already done, it may be worth your while to purchase it or put a clause in the purchase agreement that they produce it as part of the purchase of the house.

Legal Fees

Depending on where you live, you can usually choose a lawyer or notary to complete the legal paperwork relating to your mortgage. These fees can vary a lot depending on the firm you choose and the complexity of the mortgage transaction. It is best to take your phone book and do some research in order to determine who is best to do your mortgage legal work.

Fire Insurance

You need to insure your home against fire. You will be insuring the building and not the land, since it is the building that could burn down. Again, research the costs on this as it can vary.

Home Inspection Fee

With older homes, it can be worth the money to have a professional engineer inspect the house and give you a detailed report. This person will look at every possible area of the house from electrical to plumbing and roof to foundation. The report will list all the good and all the bad. It may also provide suggestions to improve the areas that need attention.

Property Taxes

Depending on when you purchase the house, you may owe the vendor property taxes or they may owe you. As discussed in a separate chapter, most property taxes are paid in July but cover the whole calendar year of January to December. So, if you purchase before July, then the vendor will owe you property taxes since they haven't been paid yet, but are still owing. If you purchase the house after July, then the vendor has paid the property taxes for the whole year and you may owe for what is remaining in the year. Let's say you bought on September 1st. Then you would owe the vendor for 4 months (September to December). This could be an added expense to you because it is money that you owe right away when you see the legal firm to sign the mortgage documents.

Land Purchase Tax

This isn't common in every province. In British Columbia, the provincial government will charge up to a 1% property purchase tax. This will depend, however, on what loan to value (LTV) your mortgage is at with the FI. The higher the LTV, the less tax, if any, you will pay. However, others will have to pay the full 1% up front. So, for a purchase of $150,000.00, that is a $1,500.00 expense.

GST on New Purchases

On a new home purchase, you will be charged the 7% GST. There is a rebate of up to a maximum of 2.5% allowed, with certain restrictions. This currently only applies to new housing and not resale housing, unless there has been a major restoration of the house.

Broker Fee

If you are using a broker to arrange your mortgage, find out what fees you will owe before you officially request that they look for a mortgage for you. If you are paying a fee, know ahead of time what it will be.

Moving Costs

Don't forget these costs. Whether you choose a professional mover or a bunch of friends with trucks to help, you will have some costs here.

Strata Maintenance Fee

If you are purchasing a condominium or townhouse, you will owe a monthly fee for the upkeep of the common areas such as rugs in the hallways, lawn maintenance or snow removal. You may be required to pay a month in advance.

Repairs to New Home

There may be items that need attention in your new home immediately. There are other items that are more cosmetic, such as repainting the interior. If you see any of these coming up, then budget for them.

How Is My Interest Rate Calculated?

$ $ $

Most mortgage interest rates compound on a "semi-annual basis not in advance." Now, that is a phrase you don't hear too often. When I took my mortgage brokers course, the conversion of interest rates was one item that required a lot of practice, study and understanding. It was the first mathematical item the course taught you and without its understanding, you wouldn't get very far in the course.

Mortgage payments are not made every six months, so why is the interest rate calculated this way? All I can say is that its the method reported on the legal paperwork. When you are quoted an interest rate or see the mortgage interest rates posted in a branch, they are usually compounding semi-annual interest rates. However, the term "semi-annual interest rate" is not stated to you. Why are they not telling you this? It's not because they are trying to hide something from you, but rather because they either don't know how to explain it to you in a simple manner or they don't know what it means themselves.

The less number of times your interest rate compounds per year the better the interest rate is to you when borrowing money. The opposite is true if your were an investor because you want your investment to compound more often to increase your rate of return. The FI's computer will do a special calculation internally to convert this semi-annual interest rate to a monthly compounding interest rate in order to produce monthly (and weekly, bi-weekly and semi-monthly) payment schedules.

The following is an attempt to show you the differences between the same interest rates compounding as a semi-annual interest rate (2 times per year) and a monthly interest rate (12 times per year). Note the difference in the payment column when comparing. This example will assume a $100,000.00 mortgage with an amortization of 25 years.

Example: Compound Semi-Annually vs. Monthly Not in Advance

Int. Rate	Compounding Period	Paym't/Month	Diff/Month Paym't
7.50%	Semi-Annually	$731.55	
7.50%	Monthly	$738.99	
	Difference		$7.44
9.00%	Semi-Annually	$827.98	
9.00%	Monthly	$839.20	
	Difference		$11.22
11.00%	Semi-Annually	$962.53	
11.00%	Monthly	$980.11	
	Difference		$17.58

It should be noted that there are mortgages that are compounded on a monthly basis, instead of semi-annually, so be careful. These mortgages are called "collateral mortgages." It should be obvious that the less number of times a mortgage interest rate compounds, the better the payment to you and the less interest you will end up paying in the end.

Not In Advance

What does that statement tacked on to the end mean? It means that the first payment isn't due until after the first month has gone by. If you were paying "in advance," then on the same day your mortgage was put into place by the FI, you would have your first mortgage payment also due. Instead, your first payment isn't due until a month later, which means "not in advance." If the mortgage for some strange reason was set up as "in advance," then your payments would be lower than with a "not in advance" mortgage because you are paying the monthly payments early. As a comparison to the above chart, the 7.50% semi-annual payment would become $727.08 if it was calculated "in advance." These are terms that your lawyer or notary should also be able to explain to you when signing your legal paperwork.

Portability & Assumption

$ $ $

This topic will interest you if you are part way through a closed term mortgage – for instance, 2 years into a 5-year closed term – and you are selling your house. There will be three choices here from which you can choose only one.

Portability

This means that you can take your mortgage terms with you to a new mortgage on a new house you are purchasing. So, if you have 3 years remaining in the 5-year term at 7.50% with $105,350.00 owing, you can transfer all of this over to the new mortgage on a new purchase at the same FI and avoid paying any penalty charges. Let's say, however, that you only need an $85,000.00 mortgage on the new house you just purchased. Most FI's will transfer over $85,000.00 of the mortgage at 7.50% with 3 years remaining in the term and only charge you an interest penalty on the difference ($105,350.00 – $85,000.00 = $20,350.00). You will have to decide if this is attractive enough for you.

If you need more money than the $105,350.00, then either an interest rate average, blending the interest rates, will be used or a split mortgage term will be suggested, if the FI offers this term type.

Assumption

This is when the person purchasing your house takes over your mortgage as it is. They will have to qualify for the mortgage at your FI. If they qualify for the mortgage, you are off the hook for any future liability. There used to be assumptions without qualifications, but this left the seller, or the vendor (you), responsible for the mortgage even though you no longer had an interest in the property. If your interest rate is lower than interest rates being offered at the time, then this may be an attractive selling feature for your house. Your Realtor will have to know this information so they can use it to market your house.

If the purchaser doesn't need the whole amount of money owing on the mortgage, you will end up paying an interest penalty on the difference; however, this is still cheaper than paying a penalty on the whole amount of money owing. If the purchaser needs more money than is owing on the mortgage, then the FI may work out either an average interest rate, which is a blended rate, or a split term mortgage type, if available.

Pay the Penalty

If neither of these other two ideas work, then you will be faced with paying the greater of a 3-month interest rate penalty or interest rate differential (IRD) on the closing date of the sale of your house (depending on the policy of your FI). There is a separate chapter on this topic entitled, "Early Renewing Your Mortgage."

Property Taxes

$ $ $

If you own real estate, which includes a mobile home with or without land, you will be required to pay property taxes, usually on an annual basis. There are a few municipalities, provinces, cities, townships, etc. where the property taxes are payable more often than annually. This chapter will discuss the collection and payment of these taxes as it relates to your mortgage.

Some property taxes can be paid on a monthly basis as an electronic debit directly from your bank account to the municipality or province. Others can be paid using telephone banking. Some give you the choice of paying the whole amount on the annual due date while others will accept post-dated cheques on a monthly basis. Finally, your FI may collect your property taxes as part of your regular mortgage payment.

Most property taxes are due annually in the middle of the year, around June/July. When you pay these taxes at this time of the year, you are actually paying 6 months in arrears and 6 months in advance. Property taxes are for the calendar year of January to December. As stated, however, they aren't due until July. January isn't viewed as a very good month to require your property taxes since most people are thinking about paying off their Christmas present bills, etc. There is no way the municipality would be able to require the full payment of property taxes at that time. Therefore, the middle of the year seems like a better alternative.

It used to be that your FI would require you to pay your property taxes as part of your mortgage payment. Your FI would then pay your property taxes for you directly in July. This way, the FI knew for certain that your taxes were up to date. If your taxes ever get behind by a few years, the municipality or city has the right to place a lien on the property and force its sale through the courts. This could affect the FI's interest in the property because the tax arrears are paid first before the FI's mortgage charge on the property. In times when property values are rising, the FI may not be as concerned about tax arrears even if the property went through a forced sale.

When interest rates are high in the marketplace, the FI is more open to collect and pay your property taxes. This money is pooled by the FI to generate income because they have to pay you a low amount of interest on your property tax account (usually around 3%) while they can make higher rates of return on this money even after the expense of paying staff to administer all their mortgage property tax accounts. When interest rates are low, however, they usually end up losing money in the administering of property taxes and, therefore, will discourage any new mortgages being set up where they will collect property taxes.

Over the years, property taxes have been going up substantially in major urban areas. If the FI is collecting your property taxes, they have to predict how much your taxes will go up a year before you or they know how much your taxes will be. Often this guess is wrong which means your mortgage property tax account may go into an overdraft state with the FI. Then comes the surprise to the customer when their property taxes are adjusted for the following year. Let me explain. Let's say your FI has been collecting your property taxes all year and there is a balance of $1,600.00 in July. However, the tax notice issued says you actually owe $2,100.00. You are $500.00 short. If you have the $500.00, then the FI would like you to pay it into your tax account with them to make up the difference. If you don't, then the FI will pay the $2,100.00 and overdraw your tax account by $500.00. They will then predict what your taxes will be for the following year, let's say $2,400.00 and add the tax overdrawn amount to this. This makes $2,900.00 ($500 + $2,400). For ease of calculations, we will assume you are paying monthly mortgage payments. For the upcoming year, instead of your property tax portion of your monthly payment being $133.33 ($1,600.00 divided by 12), it will be $241.66 ($2,900.00 divided by 12). This can be quite a shocker to the customer who wasn't expecting the $108.33 per month payment increase.

183

Another example of how you can get an overdrawn tax account is when you purchase a new house. Let's say you purchase in March and the FI will be collecting your taxes. You only have 3 months until taxes are due. Some FI's will require you to deposit sufficient funds in March to make up this difference. Others will collect for the 3 months, pay the taxes, put your tax account into arrears, make the adjustment as per the above paragraph and notify you of the change. In the following year, they may, depending on their prediction, reduce the tax portion of your payment.

It isn't that you don't owe this money, because you do. Due to this very reason, many FI's now refuse to collect property taxes. It is difficult for them to predict what your taxes will be in the next year. When they are wrong, the customer, of course, blames them for being wrong and usually an unfortunate dispute arises, which is perceived as poor customer service relations. Therefore, the FI lets customers be fully responsible for their own collection and payment of property taxes in order to avoid a potentially difficult situation with their customers.

Many FI's will provide an alternative for the collection of the property taxes without the FI actually paying the property taxes on your behalf. They will set up another account for your money to be transferred to on a monthly basis. You, not them, are fully responsible to ensure that enough funds are available at tax time, and you, not them, actually pay the property taxes when they are due. In this way, the FI is still able to make income off your savings account which the taxes are being collected into, but it doesn't have to go through the other hassles and internal costs of paying the taxes on your behalf.

If your FI is collecting your property taxes and you notice that the tax portion of your payment has gone up a lot, you should receive a notice in the mail from them explaining why it went up. However, if you still don't understand, have one of their staff explain it to you. The increase will usually be communicated to you in July or August and will either start in August or September.

So far, I have been mainly talking about increases in your mortgage payment due to property tax adjustments. There are the odd times when you will have too much in your tax account and the FI will adjust your payment downward. This isn't a usual case, however. The majority of tax accounts are either set up for the correct amount or you owe more.

Back to budgeting again for a minute. If you are responsible for the collection and payment of your property taxes, then make sure this is inputted into your budget as an expense item. Set up a separate account if possible (depending on the service charges, of course) into which the money can be either deposited or transferred. Through the use of telephone or computer banking, you can easily make this transfer yourself. When tax time comes, you then request the amount of money you want taken out of the mutual fund and have it deposited into your account for you to pay the taxes owing. As you can see, there are many alternatives when it comes to collection and payment of your property taxes.

Early Renewing Your Mortgage

$ $ $

When interest rates start to decline, the personnel at an FI receive phone call after phone call asking the same question: "Is it worth my while to early renew my mortgage, pay the penalty involved and, therefore, receive the current lower interest rate?" They are disappointed when the response is, "It depends, there is no clear cut answer to your question." I have heard it said that if there is more than a 2% spread between your mortgage interest rate and the current interest rate, then it is worth your while to pay the penalty in order to receive the better, lower, interest rate. That may or may not be true either.

What early renewing your mortgage means is this: Let's say you took a 5-year term and currently have 4 years remaining in the term until it renews. By early renewing you are breaking the old contract with the FI and choosing a new term at a lower interest rate. However, when you early renew your mortgage, there is often a penalty that you need to pay in order to break the old mortgage term contract. Usually this penalty is the greater of either 3 month's interest or interest rate differential compensation.

3 Month's Interest

Quite simply, this is the value of 3 monthly interest payments on your mortgage (not principal and interest, just the interest).

Interest Rate Differential Compensation

This is a little more complex. The pieces of the equation used are the current interest rate minus the new interest rate, how long until the current maturity and the amount of money outstanding currently. Through a complicated formula, which a computer uses, the IRD compensation is calculated. To give you an idea of how costly this can be, here are a few comparisons. Let's assume today is August 30, 1997 and your mortgage doesn't mature until August 30, 2001 (so 4 years). The current mortgage balance is $100,000.00 and your current interest rate is 10.0%. The current 5 year mortgage rate is now 9.0% which you are interested in. To obtain this better interest rate, your IRD compensation would be about $3,200.00. If the current 5 year mortgage rate was 8.0%, then the IRD would equal about $6,300.00.

What does the IRD represent? It is the difference in interest you would have normally paid over the next 4 years. In other words, the difference between 10% and 9% is 1%. This 1% difference on $100,000.00 over the next 4 years represents about $3,200.00 in interest you would have paid. In our scenario, in order to obtain that one extra year (5 years minus your current 4 years remaining) at the lower interest rate, you are paying about $3,200.00.

Is this worth while? That depends what you think interest rates will be in 4 years when your mortgage would normally mature. It usually isn't worth your while to proceed with this scenario because all you are buying is one extra year at the lower interest rate.

Most times, this makes more sense if you are in the last year of a term, interest rates are low and there is speculation that interest rates may be on the rise soon. There are various questions that you need to ask yourself. Do you believe the speculation that interest rates are going to go up? Do you believe that when your mortgage matures in less than a year interest rates are going to be higher than they are now? How much is your penalty going to be and is it worth your while to pay this penalty in order to obtain the lower interest rate? By taking the new interest rate and new term, how much interest do you really save when you net out the penalty you have to pay? How long of a term are you thinking of early renewing into, say 3-5 years? Do you believe the current interest rate and term you are planning on early renewing into will be the lowest possible over the term you are locking into? There is no use locking in for a 5-year term if you believe interest rates will be lower again in 3 years. This is the trick, however. No one knows what interest rates will be at in 6 months, 3 years or 5 years. Your decision is pure speculation about what you perceive will happen in the future. That is why this is your decision to make and the FI will not tell you what to do.

Years ago, the 5-year interest rate was sitting at 11.75%. It went down to 11.25%. Due to the uncertainty in the economy at the time, many people locked in for the 5 year term thinking this was a wise thing to do because at the time it didn't appear rates would be going down for some time. Unfortunately for these people, the interest rates did come down to record lows during the next 5 years. When their mortgages matured, they were able to get the better interest rate, but over those 5 years, they were paying more than the current rates. There is no way of knowing what interest rates are going to do from one week to another. I have seen prime rate spike up almost 2% in one day, which is a real shocker!

Blending Interest Rates

As an alternative to paying the high penalties up front, some FI's offer something called blending. Through a computer program, they will enter various data about your current mortgage plus what you would like to do. Instead of getting the current interest rate for the term you want, you will pay a higher interest rate. You are going to pay a higher interest rate over the new term chosen to offset the payment of the penalty up front. If you don't have the funds to pay the whole penalty, then this is a viable option in order to early renew and still receive a better interest rate than you are currently paying. You end up paying the penalty over the term chosen since you are paying the higher interest rate over the term.

Why Does the FI Charge a Penalty?

Consumers look at bank profits and ask why this penalty has to be charged. Most people view the penalty as a method for the FI's to line their pockets. FI's match their deposits with their loans. The spread, after costs, is their profit margin. Let's say you are holding with your FI a 10% GIC which has 3 years until maturity, and currently, the best a person can get on a GIC is 6%. How would you feel if your FI said to you, "Now that interest rates are lower, we have decided to reduce your GIC interest rate to 6% and not to compensate you for the difference of 4% over the next remaining 3 years." You would be outraged! You would at least want the extra 4% over the next 3 years paid to you if they were going to break their contract with you – correct? That's the same way it is with mortgages. Your 10% GIC is matched with a mortgage that was taken out during that time frame. If a person can lower his interest rate by early renewing and not pay a penalty, then that person can go to you, the investor who is holding the 10% GIC, and tell you that you are no longer going to be paid 10%, but instead something lower. The penalty may not seem fair at first, but it is a contract just like the investor has a contract with the FI.

What Is the Answer?

As stated at the beginning of this chapter, there is no clear cut answer to whether you should pay the penalty and early renew your mortgage. You will have to answer the various questions and come to your own conclusion. Just remember that you are making a decision about the future, which only God knows. Be content with your decision even if later it turns out to be the wrong decision, like those people who locked in at 11.25%.

Construction Mortgages

$ $ $

There are two types of construction mortgages – completion and draw mortgages. There are also two methods of building the house – builder or contractor hired and own or self-contractor.

Completion Mortgage

Most completion mortgages have the house being built by a builder or contractor. They require a one-time payment for the house once the house is 100% complete. Therefore, they only need one draw on the mortgage. The builder will self-fund the house construction from the beginning to the final stages. You may sign a contract with the builder before the house construction starts or while the house is being built. The earlier you sign the contract, the sooner you can have any say about adding or changing specific items in the house, such as kitchen cabinets or rug type and colour, etc. As the purchaser, you may have some decisions to make, although the financial responsibility doesn't start until the house is 100% complete and the FI advances the mortgage proceeds.

Draw Mortgage

You can hire a builder and do a draw mortgage or you can be your own contractor. The word "draw" means that at various stages during the construction of the home, an amount equal to the percent of work completed is advanced from the mortgage to the builder or yourself. Usually, the appraiser will either state that a specific percent is completed or a specific percent still needs to be done. There are usually 3-4 draws permitted by the FI. If doing three draws, you would receive approximately 40% of the money after the home is at lock-up, the next 30% after drywall and then a final draw, or the remaining 30%, once the house is 100% complete. However, I have seen draw mortgages go up to 7 or more draws, which can become costly. Every time a draw is requested, the appraiser will go to the house to do his report. This costs you money. The appraiser will submit his report to the FI. The FI will draw the funds off the mortgage and send them to the lawyer/notary. A state of title search is usually done by the lawyer/notary to see if there are any builder's liens against the property before the funds are released to either the builder or yourself. This also costs money.

The draws are based on the construction cost, but can also involve land cost. Some FI's will require that you own the land outright before they will proceed with the draw mortgage. Other FI's will interim finance the land purchase internally to allow you to purchase the land outright and then collect this amount owing from the final draw of the mortgage. Often there are cost overruns, so this doesn't always work out, meaning you will either have to take out a loan for the overruns or maybe even refinance the house you just built, if there is enough equity available, to pay for these overruns.

Your principal and interest repayment on the mortgage will not start until the house is 100% complete. You will be required to pay interest on the amount of funds drawn to date. Some FI's will collect this interest owing from you on a monthly basis while others will collect the interest owing from each draw when the draws are requested.

Draw mortgages are more difficult financially to put together than a completion mortgage for the simple fact that in a draw mortgage there are a lot of extra items to consider.

Builder or Contractor Hired

You will sign a contract with this person or company to build your house. If you require CMHC mortgage approval, then the contractor must be a member of the New Home Warranty program. As you have already read, this can be set up as either a completion mortgage or a draw mortgage. It is very important that you thoroughly research the builder before you sign a contract. There have been contractors who have come into a town and quickly built houses and then left before any problems started to show up. There are other horror stories out there also. Make sure you choose wisely. Unfortunately, like any industry, there are a few poor ones that tend to spoil the reputations of all the good builders.

Own or Self-Contractor

Many people believe that they can build their own house and save lots of money because they didn't have to hire and pay a professional builder to oversee the construction. If you believe this, then your FI will want to know what experience you have in the past that makes you feel competent enough to be your own contractor. Even if you have the suitable experience, do you have the time and energy. By being your own contractor, you have to research the quotes, choose the tradespeople, arrange for the trades to show up at the correct time (no sense having the painter show up when there isn't any drywall to paint), pay the trades on time, be available to complete various errands at a moment's notice, etc.

I haven't seen a self-contractor construction mortgage that isn't a draw mortgage. This means that if you don't own the land free and clear, then the FI may fund you internally for its purchase. However, the FI may require you to own the land outright before they will consider your mortgage application. The reason the land or property has to be owned by you is that once approved, a mortgage is put on the land immediately. That is why the FI can't hold the title to the land and then when the house is built put the mortgage against the land. The FI's mortgage charge is put on the state of title before any money can be drawn by you on the mortgage.

Then comes the financial pressure to pay your trades on time. Many trades will require payment immediately and will not wait until you get your next draw from your FI. Do you have enough cash available to get you from draw to draw? Again, more financial pressure in being your own contractor.

It can be very stressful being your own contractor. You will need to be very patient, flexible and organized as a person and/or as a family.

On the final page of this chapter, there is a worksheet that lists most of the items that you should be getting quotes on before visiting your FI. The FI will want a completed costing worksheet like the one provided, plus a copy of the house plans and legal description of the lot. These will be provided to the appraiser who will then determine what the market value for mortgage purposes your house comes to.

In Luke 14:28-30, Jesus is talking about the cost to a person if they want to serve Him. However, what is said has some relevance to the wisdom of preparing a cost worksheet:

> *"Suppose one of you wants to build a tower. Will he not first sit down and estimate the cost to see if he has enough money to complete it? For if he lays the foundation and is not able to finish it, everyone who sees it will ridicule him, saying, 'This fellow began to build and was not able to finish.'"*

Builder's Liens

Each province may be different on this. If a trade or supplier is not paid for its work or materials provided for your house, it can go to the expense of putting a builder's lien against your house. This lien supersedes the mortgage charge your FI has placed on the house. That is why on a draw mortgage, the FI will usually have a state of title pulled to check for any builder's liens at each draw. If there are any, then the draw will have to pay the liens first with the remainder going to the builder or yourself. In some provinces, a holdback of a specific percent of the construction cost is required for a stated time frame in case a lien is attached to the house after it is 100% complete.

CONSTRUCTION ESTIMATES –
YOU ARE YOUR OWN CONTRACTOR

Property Address:
Legal Description of Property:
Names of Owners:

		Comments:
1. Permits:	$	
2. Legal and Insurance:	$	
3. Excavation of Lot/Backfill/Trenching:	$	
4. Costs for Foundation and Footings:	$	
5. Cement Floors and Carport/Garage:	$	
6. Cement Walkways and Patios:	$	
7. Septic Field/Sewer Connection:	$	
8. Drilled Well or Water Connection:	$	
9. Framing Lumber Including Trusses:	$	
10. Labour For Framing:	$	
11. Exterior Doors and Windows:	$	
12. Fireplace, Chimney, Other Masonry:	$	
13. Roofing Supplies and Labour:	$	
14. Plumbing Fixtures, etc. and Labour:	$	
15. Electrical and Labour:	$	
16. Electrical Fixtures:	$	
17. Heating/Ventilation:	$	
18. Soffits and Eavestroughs:	$	
19. Exterior Finishings:	$	
20. Insulation:	$	
21. Drywall:	$	
22. Floor Coverings:	$	
23. Kitchen Cabinets:	$	
24. Bathroom Vanities:	$	
25. Bathroom Accessories:	$	
26. Inside Painting:	$	
27. Interior Finishing (Doors/Trim, etc.):	$	
28. Special Interior Decorating:	$	
29. Sun Deck:	$	
30. Driveway:	$	

31. Landscaping and Fencing:	$	
32. Supervision Labour:	$	
33. Extras or Other Items:	$	
34. Cost Overruns:	$	
35. Price of Lot If Don't Own Already:	$	
TOTAL:	**$**	

Transferring Your Mortgage From One FI to Another FI

$ $ $

Some FI's call this a mortgage transfer while others call it a mortgage switch. Essentially, what happens is that you are approved for your existing outstanding mortgage amount at a different FI than where the mortgage is currently at for the exact dollar for dollar amount owing at that FI. The new FI will arrange to transfer the mortgage dollar for dollar to them once you have signed their internal paperwork.

Why would you do this you ask? For one thing, it doesn't usually cost you anything to complete the transfer unless you are in the middle of a closed term which means you would have a penalty to pay to the old FI. There are many reasons for switching. You are dissatisfied with the service at the old FI, you do all your regular banking at the new FI and want the mortgage there also, you are offered a better interest rate at the new FI, etc. You will need to go through the whole approval process again at the new FI. Once approved, the new FI will take care of everything including paying off the old FI's mortgage balance.

In the FI industry, this is a method for FI's to steal mortgage market share away from the competition. There are some FI's that have attempted to protect themselves by not allowing their mortgages to be transferred to another FI while in the middle of a closed term. Therefore, be sure you ask what your mortgage's condition is on this topic when you are first approved, so you are well aware later if you choose to proceed.

Interalia Mortgages

$ $ $

Another name given this is a blanket mortgage or a mortgage that covers more than one piece of property. If a person already owns a property free and clear, which means there is no mortgage on it, and they want to purchase another piece of property but don't have the cash necessary for the down payment on the new purchase, they can consider putting a mortgage on the existing parcel of land or on both pieces of land if their existing doesn't have enough equity available. The mortgage on both pieces of land would be called an interalia mortgage. This can also work if the property you already own has a low enough mortgage to provide enough equity for the down payment. But instead of doing a separate 2nd mortgage on the existing property and a new 1st mortgage on the new purchase, an interalia mortgage will save you costs as it is one mortgage and not two. It is true that on the state of title on the existing property, it will show as a 2nd mortgage interalia and on the new purchase it will show as a 1st mortgage interalia, but you will only have one mortgage payment at the FI.

Example:

Purchase price of new property =	$120,000.00
Value of existing property =	$175,000.00
Total Value of both pieces =	$295,000.00
Mortgage on existing property =	$60,000.00
Amount of money needed =	$120,000.00
Total Amount Needed =	$180,000.00
Total Needed divided by Total Value	
$180,000.00 divided by $295,000.00	
Equals 61.00% Loan to Value (LTV)	

197

There will be certain policy restrictions regarding loan to value (LTV) here which your FI can tell you about. The advantage of an interalia mortgage is that you can still proceed with this purchase even if you don't have the cash as a down payment due to the increased equity in your existing property.

If you sell one of the properties, then the interalia mortgage will have to be paid down and that may require a new appraisal on the remaining property to keep the LTV within policy. If you sell one piece, then the legal work will partially discharge the mortgage so that the FI has no more interest in the property sold, but still has an interest in the property that remains.

Your FI will be able to advise you on this with specifics that relate to your needs.

Mobile Home Financing – Without Land

$ $ $

Many people will consider purchasing a mobile home as a starter home, for downsizing when retiring or as their life-long permanent residence. Most mobile homes without land are located in a mobile home park. You will usually pay a pad rent to a landlord, but will be responsible for all your own utilities and repairs to the mobile because you own the mobile home.

When it comes to obtaining financing for a mobile home, you will find that every FI has its own policies to follow. You will find the word "chattel" used when talking about mobile homes without land. This word means property which can be moved. You own various chattels such as vehicles, motorcycles, RV's, etc. Since the mobile home is not attached to land, it is, therefore, moveable. Hence, the mobile home is a chattel. Depending on the age and remaining life expectancy of the mobile home, you will be given one or both of the following choices for financing your purchase.

Chattel Mortgage Method

Most brand new or newer mobile homes not attached to land may be eligible for mortgage financing similar to what purchasing a house on a lot would receive. The majority of these will require mortgage insurance protection as a condition of approval by the FI. This means that the FI will obtain approval for the chattel mortgage from a mortgage insurer (see separate chapter). Once you are approved for the financing (income, debt ratios, credit bureau, etc.) and the mobile home is approved by the mortgage insurer, then the purchase can be completed.

There are reasons why you would like to do a mortgage instead of a personal loan when financing a mobile home. The first is the interest rate. Usually, the mortgage interest rates are much lower than loan interest rates. The second is amortization. Brand new mobile homes can cost quite a bit. Therefore, you will want more than 5 years to pay off the debt. The third is salability. If you are selling the mobile home, it will be more attractive to the prospective buyer if they can assume the mortgage from you.

Chattel Loan Method

Many mobile homes due to age or size (single wide compared to double wide) may not fit within the mortgage method. The only other alternative in purchasing this mobile home is by way of a personal loan. Some FI's may let the loan be amortized more than 5 years, but this is unlikely. In this scenario, you are applying for a personal loan to purchase a mobile home. Your interest rate will be higher, amortization restricted and it may be harder to sell the mobile home due to the limitedness of the financing options available to the prospective purchaser. However, there is always a market of people looking to purchase their first home or a rental home who will consider an older mobile home to meet their needs.

Mobile Home Financing – With Land

$ $ $

As the title states, this is when you purchase a mobile home that is attached to land. Just like a house is attached to the land through a foundation, the mobile home is also attached to the land through both a foundation and tie downs. By doing this, plus removing the hitch and wheels, skirting around the mobile home and putting in proper vapour barriers under the mobile home, you can obtain mortgage financing similar to that of a person with a house and land. The mobile must be considered stationary and not moveable (without a lot of work).

The age and condition of the mobile home will still be a determining factor as to what financing the FI can provide you with. Since there is land involved, this will be a mortgage and not a loan. If the remaining economic life of the mobile is 10 years, then usually the maximum amortization the FI will provide is up to 10 years, even though the mobile is attached to land. Each FI will have its own financing policies relating to mobile homes attached to land. Some will only entertain this mortgage transaction if a mortgage insurer is used. Others will finance without the mortgage insurer if the loan to value (LTV) is low.

The attractiveness of a mobile attached to land is that you will gain equity if the property value or land value increases, you are doing a mortgage here, so have both a better interest rate and mortgage features available and, depending on the real estate market, the resale of a mobile attached to land may be easier than that of a mobile not attached to land.

House Moving

$ $ $

This chapter's title may look a little strange. What is meant by "house moving" is the lifting of an older house off its foundation, moving it to another lot and placing it on a new foundation. To some of you, this may sound very strange, but on the west coast in British Columbia, there are many very good older houses from Vancouver that are recycled this way. Instead of paying for the house to be bull-dozed down, the person who bought the property saves this cost by instead selling the house for a relatively inexpensive amount to a house moving company and then building a much larger house in its place. The house mover then trucks the house to its new location and either sets it up or tries to sell the house as is to a prospective buyer. Often, the houses are barged over to Vancouver Island to various communities where the land value is much cheaper compared to the Lower Mainland.

As stated, these older houses are sold to the house mover at a reasonable price. That makes them more attractive for resale. However, there are some items you should know about if you are thinking of purchasing one of these recycled houses and will need mortgage financing.

Sometimes the house mover will have a piece of land to put the house on. Other times they will try to sell the house as it is without land. Most FI's will not finance this deal until the house is set up on a proper foundation, inspected and appraised. They will not finance the house while it is still being trucked or barged to the lot. The FI may finance only the lot or bare land up to a certain percentage loan to value (LTV = usually 50-65% maximum), but not the lot and the prospective house to be put on this lot together. So, if you purchase one of these houses, you better have enough cash to purchase the land up to the maximum LTV, get the house all set up on its foundation, often re-wire, re-plumb and re-finish both the inside and outside without needing mortgage financing. Once this work is all done, it is inspected and appraised and then the FI will consider mortgaging the house and lot.

This is why many times the house mover will have a piece of land already picked out and purchased for the house. They move the house on to the property and finish it completely. Then they will put the house on the market for sale, or rent the house out.

Many people see this as a great opportunity to purchase a house at a very reduced price. Just be aware of the expenses you will still have ahead of you and that you will have difficulty obtaining mortgage financing until the house is complete.

Mortgage Broker

$ $ $

There is an increasing number of mortgage brokers in the marketplace. Many are independent, though some work for a real estate firm or even on a commission basis with an FI. With any mortgage broker, make sure you understand who is paying the placement commission to the broker. It will be either the FI, you or some combination of both.

Independent Mortgage Brokers

The sole objective of an independent mortgage broker is to find you the best mortgage deal (interest rate, terms and conditions, prepayment options, etc.) from the FI's who will pay them a commission for placing the mortgage. Most concentrate on only finding the best interest rate, even though the other items mentioned are also very important. There are few large chartered banks that will pay such a commission to the broker, so most of this business is placed with smaller trust companies, credit unions and a few banks. If the FI will not pay the broker a commission, then they may require you to pay them a commission instead for their work in placing your mortgage request. Make sure you understand ahead of time who the broker will be trying to place your mortgage with and what fees you will need to pay for this service. They may find you the best interest rate, better than the major FI's, but at whose cost and for how much cost? Did the extra $1/8\%$ or $1/4\%$ really save you any money due to costs you will incur? Remember that these individuals make their living from placing mortgages.

If a person is having trouble finding mortgage financing, they will often approach an independent mortgage broker for assistance. You could have previous poor credit, etc. In order to place the mortgage, the broker may have to approach private funds. This means that other investors have pooled their money together to lend out, usually at higher interest rates, so that you can obtain your mortgage financing. Be careful and make sure you understand everything you are doing.

Real Estate Firm Brokers

The only difference between the independent broker and the real estate firm broker is that the real estate firm broker works out of and usually for only one real estate company. The Realtor will try to hand its customer off to the firm's mortgage broker unless the client refuses. This broker will again try their best to place the mortgage with an FI that will pay them a commission for the placement of the mortgage. The broker will work hard for you because they have the Realtor to answer to since they all work in the same real estate firm.

FI Mortgage Brokers

Over the years, many FI's have found that to meet the needs of their clientele and to maintain marketshare, they need to make their lenders more mobile and flexible to meet clients after traditional banking hours or away from the branch itself. A salesforce of self-employed commissioned salespeople has been hired and trained by the larger FI's to compete with the independents and real estate firm brokers. They work exclusively for the FI they are under contract to, with some flexibility to place mortgages elsewhere if their FI declines the mortgage application. The lender will pay the commission to the FI mortgage broker, so there is usually no placement costs to the customer.

Summary of Borrowing Money – Mortgages

$ $ $

- The mortgage application is similar to a loan application, but more time consuming. It is suggested that you be pre-approved for your mortgage before you go house-shopping.

- GDSR and TDSR are important calculations done by the FI to determine if you have enough income to support both the mortgage and other debt payments.

- Two very important words you must understand when talking about mortgages are amortization and term. There are various term types available to suit your needs.

- In retail banking, there are three main mortgage types available: conventional, insured or high ratio and collateral.

- There is a special program available to those who qualify as first time homebuyers. It allows you to purchase a home with only a 5% down payment.

- When finalizing your mortgage with your FI, you know how important payment frequency can be. The more often you make your mortgage payment, the sooner the mortgage will be paid in full which means less interest costs to you.

- When purchasing a home, there are various costs other than down payment to be aware of. Make sure you have enough money saved for these before proceeding.

- The compounding frequency of your mortgage interest rate is very important. The less number of times the interest compounds, the better it is when borrowing money.

• When selling your house, you have two choices to consider to avoid any interest penalty – either portable the interest rate to your new mortgage at the same FI or offer the purchaser of your house the option to assume the mortgage at your FI. Otherwise, if you are in a fixed or closed term, the only other choice is to pay the penalty.

• Every homeowner will have to pay property taxes. Make sure you understand how your FI will be calculating your property taxes if they are collected with your regular mortgage payment.

• If you early renew your mortgage, you will most likely pay a penalty. Whether it is worth your while is a tough choice only you can make.

• A construction mortgage can be very complicated and somewhat stressful. Only brave building your own home if you have lots of patience and are organized.

• Mobile home financing has certain restrictions whether land is attached or not.

SECTION FIVE

Wills, Wealth & Whatever

$ $ $

Topics in this next section cover from wills to managing wealth to whatever may happen in the future of Canadian finance.

Command those who are rich in this present world not to be arrogant nor to put their hope in wealth, which is so uncertain, but to put their hope in God, who richly provides us with everything for our enjoyment. Command them to do good, to be rich in good deeds, and to be generous and willing to share. In this way they will lay up treasures for themselves as a firm foundation for the coming age, so that they may take hold of the life that is truly life.

1 Timothy 6:17-19

Wills & Estate Planning

$ $ $

Before I went to Bolivia, South America when I was 16 years old for a short term summer missions trip, I completed a will. I didn't have a lot at that age, but I did have a few small assets that I wanted disbursed in a certain way if by chance I didn't return home. I was preparing for the unknown future. As you can see, I made it home, although the Lord did spare my life a few times during that trip. No one knows the hour when we will be called home to glory, so it is better to be prepared now because it will be too late later to do anything about it.

Who Should Have a Will?

When a couple has children, it is essential that a will be put into place for each spouse, if for no other reason than to let everyone know who you want to take care of your children. Otherwise, in many provinces, the state (or government) assumes this role and makes the decision of guardianship in your place since you left no directions. As a Christian, this could be very unsettling since we are raising our children with Christian morals and godly principles as found in the Bible. Do you really think the world or courts will care if your child is placed in another Christian home?

Even if you are single, a will should be written up so that your assets are dealt with properly. You may want certain people to have certain treasured items and have the other assets sold with the proceeds going towards a particular charity. If you don't write a will, then no one will know and they'll be left to guess your intentions.

If you are older, you should have a will in place that you have reviewed recently to ensure that it is current. Your current will may have been drawn up 10 years ago. A lot can happen in 10 years.

Changes may need to be made. An example could be that you now want to divide your estate into six equal pieces with four portions going to each of your four children, one portion being divided equally among the grandchildren and the final portion being donated to your favourite Christian organization or charity that means something special to you. If your will doesn't say what you want, then it won't happen. Make sure your will is current. Read it again soon.

Who Do I Seek Help From?

Most FI's these days have their own trust company. Most trust companies will provide a free consultation with an expert, who is usually a professional (sometimes a lawyer), trained specifically in Estate Planning and the laws surrounding wills. The trust company's target market is customers who have higher net worths; however, they will usually sit down, free of charge, with any of their customers for a half hour discussion. You can also visit your lawyer (or notary where it is permissible) to discuss your will arrangements.

Ask if your trust company or lawyer has a workbook specifically designed to help you prepare your will. In Canada, a large part of the population, called the "baby boomers," is approaching retirement as their parents are nearing the end of their life on earth. There could potentially be a large sum of wealth being passed from one generation to the next. Therefore, estate planning and wealth management is seen as an important growth business, since wealth is going to be changing hands and the ones leaving the wealth want to make sure their wishes are followed through as stated in their will, and the ones receiving the wealth will be seeking financial advice on what to do with the wealth. Therefore, FI's, particularly the trust companies, investment dealers and financial planners, are very interested in providing products and services in estate planning and wealth management.

Who Am I On Paper?

If you obtain a workbook, you will see pages of space ready for you to fill in the blanks. You will be spending valuable time gathering information about yourself. This may seem time consuming, but it is a very important task. You will list all of your personal contacts, insurance policies, your children, special beneficiaries/charities, where documents can be found (ie. safe deposit box) and your assets (where located) and liabilities, plus other information like pre-arranged funeral arrangements.

Who Do I Want To Give My Estate To?

If you thought filling in blanks about yourself was difficult, now the decisions have to be made. When you die, how do you want your estate to be distributed? Prayerfully consider your decisions. Your family is a definite consideration, but are there other areas of need that you could help fulfill? Consider various Christian organizations such as a Christian camp, church organization, world relief organization or a charity that means something special to you. Every province has specific laws about who must be included in your will. That is where you will need to get a professional involved. Some decisions will be easy and others will prove to be difficult.

The whole task may seem mentally overwhelming because emotionally you may feel somewhat morbid thinking about your own death. It is better for you to decide ahead of time than let the courts decide what your last intentions were. Also, those left behind will have less heartache if your will, which is really a plan or map, is all laid out and all they have to do is follow it and execute your wishes. When someone dies, you may have heard others whisper the expression, "He would have wanted it that way." With a will in place, there will be no questions about the way you wanted it to be.

Who Should Be My Executor or Co-Executor?

Now for the biggest decision regarding your will. Who do you want the executor to be? The executor has a very large responsibility (see the next chapter). You are entrusting this person with specific powers that will allow your estate to be administered and disbursed (or executed) to the beneficiaries as per your directions left in your will. It is not a role to be taken lightly. It will be demanding on their time, stress level and ability to understand and administer the complexities that may come up. Not everyone is suited to be an executor. You may have a family member or a very good friend that you are fond of and, for sentimental reasons, want to be your executor.

Review and study what they must do as an executor and match their skills, abilities and gifts to the duties and responsibilities of an executor. As always, pray about your decisions and seek God's direction.

You can appoint one executor or more than one co-executor. You could have a family member being a co-executor with the trust company or your lawyer, for example. This means that the others listed as co-executors are there to assist in the administration and disbursement of your estate. This can be a very good idea, especially if you foresee family conflicts or that the executor chosen could fill some but not all of the responsibilities. Sometimes a spouse will appoint the other spouse plus a co-executor. This could be a great idea, especially if the remaining spouse is not familiar with financial related information and/or could have difficulty dealing with your absence and thus be unable to fill their duties without assistance. Think about this ahead of time.

The executor and co-executors are paid for their services from the estate. The exact amount or percentage of the estate payable is different in each province. Many people may think this is unnecessary, but read the various responsibilities of an executor and you will see that it is a lot of work and commitment. Due to this fee, the trust companies are very interested in being the executor or co-executor of a will that has a positive estate worth. The trust company has been (depending how long the trust company has been in existence, of course) executor or co-executor of numerous wills and has the experience, expertise and personnel available to carry out the powers and responsibilities of an executor in a very professional and efficient manner. If you are going to list a trust company as executor or co-executor, it is a must that you meet with their Wills Consultant and have them help draw up your will as per your wishes. They will often keep a copy of your will on file in their vault also.

Last Thoughts About Wills

No matter how you decide to set up your will, make sure you put the time necessary into gathering information, deciding how your estate is to be disbursed and who your executor or co-executor(s) are going to be. Your will is a very important document filled with valuable and useful information about what your intentions are when you are not here to see these intentions through yourself. As you can see, there are a lot of other people involved in your decisions. Seek God's wisdom.

In case you are wondering, wills are mentioned in the Bible. Hebrews 9:16-17 says:

In the case of a will, it is necessary to prove the death of the one who made it, because a will is in force only when somebody has died; it never takes effect while the one who made it is living.

Some of the Responsibilities of the Executor

$ $ $

- *Knowledge:*   The executor will need knowledge in many different disciplines, including law, accounting, taxation, banking, real estate and insurance, to name a few.

- *Impartiality:*   They cannot take sides even if they have a bias towards one viewpoint in the event of a family dispute over the will. Their decisions, based on the powers you grant them, could even strain their relationships with others whether listed or not listed in your will.

- *Time:*   A large time commitment is needed to see that all creditors are paid, estate assets are sold or transferred, taxes are filed and paid on time, various assets of the estate are invested, payment of estate funds is made to the beneficiaries or the guardian(s) of the children, etc.

- *Health:*   This is an important consideration if you are choosing an older executor. When they were younger, stress wasn't an issue, but now that they are older, can they handle the stress involved? Are they more interested in enjoying their retirement than completing your last wishes? Are they only saying yes to being your executor out of a desire to please you due to your long friendship or because you have always been the closest siblings?

- *Trust:*   You must be able to trust whomever you choose because they are entrusted with your last wishes.

They must see your will through to its end and that could take years depending on how complex your will is.

- *Experience:*   Any errors as an executor could be very costly to both the estate and to the executor.

- *Administrator:*   The executor must be able to keep track of many items at the same time in an organized manner.

- *Inter-Personal:*   They must be fair, considerate and a listener. The
  Skills: executor may be dealing with guardians, real estate brokers, bankers, lawyers, accountants and beneficiaries listed in the will.

This is not an all-inclusive list of responsibilities. There are other duties the executor may have depending on what transpires. How many of us can fill this list? That is why you must prayerfully consider who you choose as the executor or co-executor of your will. You should consider approaching your first choice and discussing with them the responsibility you are leaving them with. Review the above responsibilities with them and gain their commitment. If they are not sure, then you need to consider someone else. Just because they are your best friend doesn't mean they will be the best executor. Consider the option of a co-executor also.

A will needs an executor and an executor needs the skills, abilities and gifts to see that the will is followed to its completion properly. Indeed, a very large responsibility.

217

Wealth Management – Biblical Perspective

$ $ $

The Bible doesn't say that wealth in itself is bad or sinful. Look at how rich God made King Solomon. However, there are many examples in the Bible of how wealth has destroyed people. It is how a person handles wealth that is important here. If you are a Christian, you know that no matter how difficult this life may appear, there awaits for you in heaven wealth like you can't imagine when we meet our Creator. Imagine, streets made of gold. Can you imagine a mile of the Trans Canada Highway paved in gold?

Jesus talks about how difficult it will be for a rich man to enter the kingdom of God (Matt. 19:16-30). Why? Because this man is rich? No, because the riches on earth can create wants, desires and pleasures that are worldly in nature and that often cloud the real reason we are here on earth, which is to glorify and serve our Creator. That doesn't mean that God won't allow Christians to be wealthy. However, it does mean those who are wealthy have a great responsibility to ensure that they are accountable to God for all that He has given them.

Whatever your definition of "wealthy" is on earth, we are each accountable to God for what He has given us in our lives. In the Bible, Paul states that we are to *be joyful always; pray continually; give thanks in all circumstances, for this is God's will for you in Christ Jesus* (1 Thess. 5:16-18). Read also Luke 12:13-21 where Jesus tells the parable of the rich fool. God is definitely in control. There are many other references to wealth in the Bible, but this book's mandate (re-read the Preface) is not to delve into biblical interpretation of money and wealth. However, since this book is directed towards Christians, this topic needs to have some biblical insights.

As in the early church, we are also responsible to each other as Christians for all that God has given to us. In Acts 4:32-37, a detailed

218

description is provided about how the believers unselfishly and sacrificially gave from what they had to both provide for the needs of other believers and also to help in the furtherance of the Gospel. Not for self glorification, but for the glory of God they gave liberally.

If you are considered wealthy as per earthly standards, pray for wisdom and guidance on how God would have you glorify Him with all that He has given to you. Put God in control of everything in your life, including your finances, and you will see many blessings greater than anything you could buy on this earth. Read and meditate on one of my favourite verses in the Old Testament, Proverbs 3:5-6: *Trust in the Lord with all your heart and lean not on your own understanding; in all your ways acknowledge Him, and He will direct your paths.*

Wealth Management – Growth Industry

$ $ $

As stated in the chapter about wills, managing wealth is going to be a growth industry in the world's view. Every FI and financial advisor is gearing up to be ready and willing to help you manage your wealth. I am talking about worldly wealth here and the definition the world puts on wealth. There is expected to be a lot of wealth changing hands over the next 10-20 years from parents to children. If you have money to invest and need direction, then your FI and financial advisor would love the opportunity to show you how they are now ready to serve your needs in managing this wealth for you. In particular, the FI's see wealth management as a welcomed opportunity and will be eager to capitalize on it.

This specialized service does come at a cost. However, since this field will have quite a few competitors, the fees involved should become reasonable. You will need to evaluate whether the costs involved will be more than offset by the benefits received. There are various services you can select from to tailor-make this service to meet your needs. You may want one service such as portfolio management, but don't need other services such as day-to-day banking services, which includes paying all your bills on time for you from your account. You choose what you want and pay for what you choose.

Since this is a growth industry, the financial industry will be creating products and services that will meet the needs of the wealthy customer as they see these needs arise. What I am talking about here is more than phoning your stock broker to make a trade. All of your wealth will be managed under one portfolio for you. You can be actively involved in the decision-making or you can give specific direction and have others be in charge of your portfolio. Taxation, custodial and estate planning services can also be provided as part of your investment strategy.

In financial circles, financial planning and identifying customer's financial needs are becoming big topics of discussion. Due to the lack of real financial education of most Canadians who will eventually fit into this wealth bracket, the financial industry sees the opportunity to provide a service to meet this need while at the same time making adequate profits for themselves. Therefore, the financial industry workforce must educate themselves for this growth industry. Inquire about what services are available to help you manage your wealth. Talk with your FI or financial advisor. You may be doing just fine on your own, but it is important to keep informed about what is available.

Be sure you are comfortable with any plan, analysis or decisions put before you. There is a certain trust factor that comes into play here because you are trusting others to invest your wealth. As discussed in the previous chapter, be careful what you do with your wealth. As an example, your advisor may suggest that you not put so much money into charitable donations because it puts you above your allowable limit for taxation purposes. However, if God is directing you to give above and beyond, then I would suggest you follow His advice first, the wisdom He has given you second and the human advisor last. Always keep your priorities straight.

Canada's Financial System: Where We Have Been & Where We Are Going

$ $ $

This is the start of the "whatever" in this section. To understand where we seem to be heading in the Canadian financial marketplace, it is vital we first understand where we have come from.

Since the '80s, there have been changes made by the Federal Government relating to what is referred to as the four pillars of Canada's financial industry. Many old bank buildings were built with large pillars as part of the building's front façade, as shown on the cover of this book. This was to show their strength to the Canadian public. Imagine four of these pillars holding up the building's roof with the following written on each individual pillar:

PILLAR #1	PILLAR #2	PILLAR #3	PILLAR #4
Banks	Trust Companies	Brokerage Companies	Insurance Companies

It used to be that any one pillar could not own another pillar. They all worked together, but independent of each other. Various legislation has been changed over the years so that now each pillar can own any of the other pillars. That is why the big banks in Canada have their own trust company, brokerage company and most own an insurance company. The financial services industry has been and continues to consolidate into larger and larger "groups." Soon, in Canada, all financial products and services will be offered at a "one-stop shopping financial centre."

However, this is not all that is happening. The big banks have always enjoyed competing with each other in Canada over many years. You will continue to read about how one bank or FI beat the

222

FI's must improve their profits (bottom line), increase return on equity and be ready to make quick changes in how they conduct their business. To do this, they have to do three things. First, reduce costs which means reduce staff, close obsolete branches and push for customers to do their banking using alternate distribution methods such as bank machines, telephone banking and PC banking. Second, determine who their key markets are both in Canada and globally. Then concentrate on making the most profit possible from these markets. Third, keep ahead of their competition. Therefore, reduce expenses, improve return on equity and increase market share. That is the way it is with any business if you want to survive. However, to the consumer, there aren't as many FI's to choose from if they consolidate. That means if you don't fit the particular market which the FI is trying to attract and grow, then be prepared for some uncertainty.

You may be asking how this fits in with the Bible and especially the end times according to the Book of Revelation. Actually, it fits quite nicely. You see, the consolidation and control of commerce and the banking system are key elements of the end times. Therefore, the fact that the banking system wants to consolidate both in Canada and around the world fits. Also, the fact that most FI's around the world are working towards a cashless society, whether they will admit it publicly or not, also fits.

Therefore, don't be surprised if you hear that the unthinkable is happening in the financial services industry in Canada or around the world. It is all part of a plan that we don't control, but of which we are definitely a part.

Final Thoughts

$ $ $

As a writer, I have to accept that what has been written here will change because information is very timely. We all face changes and time limitations in our lives which can cause increased amounts of stress.

Stress in the workforce is building daily. There is stress in not knowing if we can find employment or if we can keep our existing job(s). No longer does the worker or the company expect any loyalty from each other. Gone are the days of the 30 years of service and the gold watch treatment. It is expected that you may work for many different employers over your lifetime. Sometimes you will be working two or more part-time jobs at the same time, instead of one full-time job. Of course, the employer's expectation of their employees may seem unrealistic at times, but the employer appears to be in control of the worker. This means that you must be constantly preparing yourself in your area of expertise or be educating yourself in a new discipline to keep ahead of change. Of course, this cuts into your time. Some people have opted to work for themselves, being self-employed. With constant downsizing of the workforce by all companies in Canada, there has been an increase in the self-employed workforce. All of this can cause added stress because you are really in charge of your own destiny, no one else is going to take care of you, so all your time and effort is centered on work for survival.

Stress can also lead to health problems, financial difficulties or family hardship. Each of these can then lead to each other or some other problem, unless we do something and we do it fast to keep our sanity and our lives together.

Each of us needs a coping mechanism to help us handle the stress load of dealing with change and time limitations. For a starting point, if you are a Christian, might I suggest you pray about whatever changes are happening in your life and share it with God. He is our comforter. Also, prayerfully help each other. Be available to talk, encourage and pray with each other. Meditate on God's Word.

If you are not a Christian or have any uncertainties, you need the salvation offered through Jesus Christ. Seek out a friend who is a Christian or talk with a pastor of an evangelical church. Without Christ, all your earthly coping mechanisms will fail and you will have no eternal security, which is more important than anything else this world has to offer.

We all need a great awakening to God in our spiritual lives to help us cope with our day-to-day Christian living.

Summary of Wills, Wealth & Whatever

$ $ $

- A will is a very important document which everyone should have completed to provide direction for the executor and your loved ones.

- Read through the various responsibilities of the executor. Prayerfully consider who should be the executor or co-executors of your will.

- Wealth in itself is not evil. What we do with our wealth and our motives are what lead to either good or evil. We are accountable to God as Christians for all He gives us.

- In the world, wealth management is seen as a growth industry. The financial industry is getting itself ready to provide specialized service, financial planning and products to this market. Always take God's leading first in any financial decisions.

- The Canadian financial system has changed dramatically just as other industries have also gone through changes. Be prepared for continued change as the financial industry attempts to compete globally as well as at home.

- The changes in the financial industry around the world fit in with what the Bible teaches about the end times in the Book of Revelation. Don't be surprised.

- Constant change and time management can cause immense amounts of stress in our lives. Prepare yourself for the future, but first get yourself on track with God.

- As Christians, we often need a great awakening to God and His Son, Jesus Christ. If you haven't received God's greatest gift of salvation, you need to deal with the uncertainties of eternity first before dealing with life's daily uncertainties.

Appendix

$ $ $

The following are various worksheets that are found in this book which may be used for your personal use only. Permission to photocopy them is granted for your personal use; however, they are not to be used as an instructional tool.

In a one month time-frame:

Banking Item Costing:	#	Cost/Item	Total $	
# of cheques written				
# of withdrawals made (live teller)				
# of withdrawals made (automation)				
# of bills paid (live teller)				
# of bills paid (automation)				
# of transfers of $ from this acct				
# of electronic transfers/debit memos				
# of money orders/bank drafts				
# of times used another FI's bank machine				
# of times bought goods electronically				
# of times purchased traveller's cheques				
# of times charged for overdraft protection				
# of certified cheques				
Is there any record keeping fee on the acct?				
If statement, do you pay each month for it?				
Do you pay for cancelled cheques returned?				
Other items:				
#				
#				
#				
#				
#				
Total Cost per Month: (A)	#=		$	(A)
Account Service Package Cost at FI:			$	
Extra items above Service Package:				
#				
#				
#				
#				
#				
Total Cost per Month (B)			$	(B)
Subtract (B) from (A) to get (C)	(A)=			
	(B)=			
	(C)=			

If (C) is negative then stay with the pay as you go per item method.
If (C) is positive then consider changing to the service package method.

Chequing Account Reconciliation for the Time Frame of: _____			
Last Balance	$_____	(A)	
Itemize each Credit/Deposit/ECM, etc.:			
*	$		
*	$		
*	$		
*	$		
*	$		
*	$		
*	$		
*	$_____		
Subtotal:	$	$_____	(B)
Add (A) plus (B) to get (C):		$	(C)
Itemize each Debit/Withdrawal/EDM, etc.:			
*	$		
*	$		
*	$		
*	$		
*	$		
*	$		
*	$		
*	$		
*	$		
*	$		
*	$		
*	$		
*	$		
*	$_____		
Subtotal:	$	$_____	(D)
Take (C) and subtract (D) to get (E):		$	(E)

Compare (E) to your cheque register balance.

BUDGET WORKSHEET

Budget for the Pay Period of: _____

Income Items:			Commitment Corner:		
	$				
	$				
	$				
	$				
Total Income	$				

Expense Items:	Budget	Actual	Running Tally:		
	$	$	Expense Item:		
	$	$		$	$
	$	$		$	$
	$	$		$	$
	$	$		$	$
	$	$	On-going Total	$	$
	$	$			
	$	$	Expense Item:		
	$	$		$	$
	$	$		$	$
	$	$		$	$
	$	$		$	$
	$	$	On-going Total	$	$
	$	$			
	$	$	Expense Item:		
	$	$		$	$
	$	$		$	$
	$	$		$	$
	$	$		$	$
Total Expenses	$	$	On-going Total	$	$

Savings Items:	Budget	Actual			
	$	$	Summary	Budget	Actual
	$	$	Total Income=	$	$
	$	$	Total Expenses=	$	$
	$	$	Total Savings=	$	$
	$	$	End Result (+/-)	$	$
Total Savings	$	$			

CREDIT APPLICATION WORKSHEET

PERSONAL INFORMATION:

_____ _____ _____ _____ _____
Last Name   First Name   Initial   Social Insurance Number   Birth Date (Y/M/D)

Mailing/Physical Address:

_____
Box/Apt./Suite/R.R. #   Street # and Name   City   Prov.   Postal Code

How long have you lived at this address? _____ years.
If less than 3 years, please state previous addresses:

_____ = _____ years.
_____ = _____ years.

Home Phone #: (____) ____ - _____ Work Phone #: (____) ____ - _____

_____ _____ _____ _____ _____
Spouse's Last Name   First   Initial   Social Insurance Number   Birth Date (Y/M/D)

EMPLOYMENT INFORMATION:

_____
Employer's Name   Your Occupation   Phone Number   Years Employed

What is your gross monthly income? $_____
Are you F/T, P/T, Casual or Seasonal? _____
Are you self-employed? _____ (Y/N) If so, for how long? _____ years.
If less than 5 years at present employer, please list previous employers:

_____

_____
Employer's Name   Your Occupation   Phone Number   Years Employed

Spouse's Employment:

_____
Employer's Name   Your Occupation   Phone Number   Years Employed

What is your gross monthly income? $_____
Are you F/T, P/T, Casual or Seasonal? _____
Are you self-employed? _____ (Y/N) If so, for how long? _____ years.

Other Sources of Income:

_____
Source of Income (Pension/RIF/Rental income, etc.)   Monthly Income Amount

YOUR PERSONAL ASSETS, LIABILITIES AND NET WORTH

List all personal bank accounts:

Financial Institution	Bank Account #	Balance $	Chequing/Savings

Assets:			
Total Cash in Bank Accounts:		$	*Any other details about*
Listing of Stocks/Bonds/Mutual Funds:			*Assets can be written here if*
*		$	*not enough room available:*
*		$	
Term Deposits/Savings Bonds			
*		$	
*		$	
RSP's (where and maturity date):			
*		$	
*		$	
Other Investments (provide details):			
*		$	
Automobiles-Personal (Yr/Make/Model):			
*		$	
*		$	
Other Assets-Collectibles, Furnishings:			
*		$	

Real Estate			
Principal Residence Present Value: $		**Mortgage**	
How much is owing on mortgage? $		Monthly Payment Amt:	$
Where is mortgage? _____		Monthly Property Taxes:	$
If have 2nd mortgage, how much? $		Strata Fee (condo):	$
Where is 2nd mortgage? _____		What is your interest rate?	%
Value of house after mortgages:	$	When is maturity date?	
Rental Property Present Value: $		Monthly Payment Amt:	$
How much is owing on mortgage? $		Monthly Property Taxes:	$
Where is mortgage? _____		Strata Fee (condo):	$
Value of house after mortgage:	$	When is maturity date?	
Other Real Estate Owned (details):			
*		$	
TOTAL ASSETS		$	

Liabilities:	Balance	Monthly Payment	Any collateral held against this debt?
List your Credit Cards:			
*	$	$	
*	$	$	
*	$	$	
List any Personal Loans:			
*	$	$	
*	$	$	
*	$	$	
List any Personal Line of Credit:			
*	$	$	
*	$	$	
Other Debts You Have:			
*	$	$	
*	$	$	
From Assets Section:			
Bal. owing Principal Residence	$	$	Full Monthly Paym't
Bal. owing Principal Residence 2nd	$	$	Full Monthly Paym't
Bal. owing Rental Property	$	$	Full Monthly Paym't
Rent/Room & Board/Other		$	
Total Liabilities & Total Paym'ts	**$**	**$**	

Net Worth:	
Total Assets	$
Minus Total Liabilities	$
Equals Net Worth	$

What credit product are you applying for? _____

How much money do you need? _____

How soon do you need this financing? _____

Is this application in your name only or jointly with spouse? _____

If you were to need a co-signor (who is equally as responsible for your loan as you are), who would that person be? _____

Any other information you feel is useful towards this credit application?

_____

THE ABC'S OF DEBT SERVICE RATIO CALCULATION WORKSHEET

STEP 1: What Is the Total Income Being Used?

Turn into annualized income (therefore, if paid monthly, multiply by 12, if bi-weekly multiply by 26, etc.)

Applicant #1 income = $_____ x _____ = $_____ /year
Applicant #2 income = $_____ x _____ = $_____ /year

Total annualized income   = $_____ /year (A)

STEP 2: What Is the Total Mortgage Amount Going To Be?

Purchase Price of House $_____ (B)
Less: Down payment $_____
Equals Mortgage Amount of $_____ (C)

STEP 3: What Is the Loan To Lending Value Ratio?

Take (B) above and divide it by (C) above: _____ /_____ =_____ %
                                             (B)   (C)   (D)

STEP 4: What Are Mortgage Payments On This?

Go to your personal computer and input the amount of mortgage, amortization, interest rate, term if asked, and ensure that the interest rate compounds semi-annually not in advance (or # compound frequencies = 2). Use the monthly payment in our calculations even if you plan on paying bi-weekly, etc.

Write here what your monthly mortgage payment will be _____ and multiply it by 12 to get an annualized mortgage payment = _____ (E)

STEP 5: What Is the Gross Debt Service Ratio (GDSR)?

Add Together:

1) the annualized mortgage payment found in **(E)** $_____

2) the annualized property taxes $_____

3) the space heating costs (usually $900/year) $_____

4) 1/2 of condo or maintenance fee $_____

Total $_____ **(F)**

Write down the total annualized income as found in **(A)** above $_____
(A)

Divide **(F)** by **(A)** to get the GDSR % _____ /_____ = _____ %
(F)   **(A)**   **(G)**

STEP 6: What Is the Total Debt Service Ratio (TDSR)?

Annualize all of your other monthly debts including loan payments, LOC payments and credit card payments.

Item:

_____ $_____

_____ $_____

_____ $_____

_____ $_____

_____ $_____

_____ $_____

_____ $_____

Total of all other annualized debt $_____ **(H)**

Add to **(H)** the total found in **(F)** $_____ **(F)**

This gives you total of all debts $_____ **(J)**

Now divide **(J)** by **(A)** to get the TDSR: _____ /_____ = _____ %
(K)   **(J)**   **(A)**

STEP 7: Now Does It Fit?

GDSR = _____ (G)
TDSR = _____ (K)

Further Notes:

CONSTRUCTION ESTIMATES –
YOU ARE YOUR OWN CONTRACTOR

Property Address:
Legal Description of Property:
Names of Owners:

		Comments:
1. Permits:	$	
2. Legal and Insurance:	$	
3. Excavation of Lot/Backfill/Trenching:	$	
4. Costs for Foundation and Footings:	$	
5. Cement Floors and Carport/Garage:	$	
6. Cement Walkways and Patios:	$	
7. Septic Field/Sewer Connection:	$	
8. Drilled Well or Water Connection:	$	
9. Framing Lumber Including Trusses:	$	
10. Labour For Framing:	$	
11. Exterior Doors and Windows:	$	
12. Fireplace, Chimney, Other Masonry:	$	
13. Roofing Supplies and Labour:	$	
14. Plumbing Fixtures, etc. and Labour:	$	
15. Electrical and Labour:	$	
16. Electrical Fixtures:	$	
17. Heating/Ventilation:	$	
18. Soffits and Eavestroughs:	$	
19. Exterior Finishings:	$	
20. Insulation:	$	
21. Drywall:	$	
22. Floor Coverings:	$	
23. Kitchen Cabinets:	$	
24. Bathroom Vanities:	$	
25. Bathroom Accessories:	$	
26. Inside Painting:	$	
27. Interior Finishing (Doors/Trim, etc.):	$	
28. Special Interior Decorating:	$	
29. Sun Deck:	$	
30. Driveway:	$	

31. Landscaping and Fencing:	$	
32. Supervision Labour:	$	
33. Extras or Other Items:	$	
34. Cost Overruns:	$	
35. Price of Lot If Don't Own Already:	$	
TOTAL:	$	